The Camden Town Murder

GREAT MURDER TRIALS OF THE TWENTIETH CENTURY

The Camden Town Murder

by
SIR DAVID NAPLEY

St. Martin's Press
New York

Library of Congress Cataloging-in-Publication Data

Napley, David Sir, 1915–
    The Camden Town murder.

    1. Wood, Robert, b. 1879.   2. Crime and criminals—
England—Biography.   3. Dimmock, Emily Elizabeth,
1884–1907.   4. Murder—England—Case studies.   5. Trials
(Murder)—England—Case studies.   I. Title.
HV6248.W73N36   1987   364.1′523′0942142   87-13104
ISBN 0-312-01157-1

First published in Great Britain by George Weidenfeld & Nicolson
Limited.

First U.S. Edition

10 9 8 7 6 5 4 3 2 1

Robert Wood
(*From a drawing by Joseph Simpson*)

Foreword

A good story is the combination of many things. It needs not only drama and interest, but must reflect the whole vivid tapestry of human behaviour, sometimes dramatic, sometimes sad, often happy and frequently surprising. The story must be such that, as it unfolds, one leaves the foot of each page eager to commence the page which follows.

Works of pure fiction, therefore, demand not only literary talent but a vivid imagination coupled with a special depth of human understanding. Yet the best stories of all are those which do no more than record life itself, and where has that been better portrayed, over the years, than in the courts of law? Drama, poignancy, humour, mystery, histrionics, courage, cowardice, violence and kindness are all to be found there for the taking.

This book, intended as the first of a series, aims to present in story form the actual facts, circumstances and happenings which culminated in what has become known as the Camden Town murder trial of the year 1907.

The Camden Town murder case, apart from its special interest as a story, presents a number of features which single it out from other murder trials. For a long time, until the end of the nineteenth century, an accused person was not able to give evidence on his own behalf. Wood was the first defendant to do so in a murder trial after the change in the law which made this possible. Whether or not it would be wise to call him to the witness box involved a difficult and dramatic decision. The trial itself came at a crucial point in the career of Sir Edward Marshall Hall KC, and his conduct of the trial is as interesting a subject for critical appraisal as the conduct before and during the trial of the accused himself. In short, this was truly a *cause célèbre*. Each succeeding day of the murder trial unfolded to the public a story as enthralling as any novel, as dramatic as any play and as intriguing and mystifying as any detective story. In those days murder was a capital offence, and, denied radio and television, the interest of the public was riveted by the daily struggle described in the press. Every facet was reported: the endeavours of the police, probing and dissecting the facts as they were uncovered; the prosecution seeking to establish damning charges; the greatest advocate of the day, Edward Marshall Hall KC, desperately fighting for the life of the accused; in the background the angel of death hovering over the gallows. The public was transfixed by the drama at the Central Criminal Court.

The daily press reports and the transcript of the evidence given at the Old Bailey trial provided the essential facts. They did not, however, weld the events into a coherent story. I have endeavoured to restore continuity, by looking back, almost eighty years later, reconstructing what seems to have occurred and, where there are gaps, drawing on my imagination only for meetings and events which, while unrecorded by the evidence, appear likely to have happened. This apart, I have adhered strictly to the facts, while striving to give form to the characters, legal and lay, who were involved, and to explain the part played by those characters, especially the lawyers.

I wish to express my gratitude for information and extracts from *The Trial of Robert Wood*, edited by Basil Hogarth, published by Thorton Butterworth, 1936, reproduced by permission of Associated Book Publishers; to Victor Gollancz Ltd for use of the admirable *The Life of Sir Edward Marshall Hall KC* by the late Edward Marjoribanks; to Harrap & Company for *The Life of Sir Travers Humphries* by Douglas Brown; to the *News of the World* for extracts from their contemporaneous reports; to my daughters for helpful suggestions; to my secretary Deanne Potts for a great deal of typing; and to my publishers for their ready assistance.

David Napley

The Camden Town
Murder

Chapter I

London, 1905: the South African War receding into history; Gladstone gone; the Conservative Government tottering to dissolution; German might developing to alarming proportions.

Into St Pancras Station steamed the Sheffield Express. Five carriages along, in the restaurant car, Bertram Shaw placed the last stack of dishes in the last remaining space, grabbed his overcoat and made for home. Bertram Shaw, Bert to his intimates, had 'cooked' his way up and down the lines of the Midland Railway for many years. It was a tedious pastime and, when he left the heat of the kitchen at the end of a run, he felt he had earned his rest, to say nothing of his glass of bitter. But if those were his thoughts as he clambered from the carriage, by the time he had walked the Euston Road he had decided that the bitter deserved earlier attention.

Bert had stood in that day for one of his friends, so he had arrived at St Pancras in the evening rather than at 11.30 in the morning, which was his usual time. Moreover, the train had been on time, and the warmth of a saloon bar was to be preferred to the lonely room in the netherland of Camden Town. Turning out of the enveloping evening mist, away from the scurrying feet of workers returning to their homes, through the swing doors of the Duke's Arms, he made his way to the fire, warmed his hands and called for his 'usual'.

Bert brought his pint to a table near the fire and took his evening paper from his pocket.

'Going to be foggy,' said the landlord as he wiped the bar.

'Yes,' replied a customer on the next table, 'I may as well pack up for tonight. This sort of weather chills yer bones.'

1

Bert looked up. The speaker, a young girl of about twenty-five years of age, was somewhat painted and rather gaudily dressed. Seeing Bert looking at her the girl smiled and drew her chair closer to the fire.

'I think I'll never get warm again,' she said.

'What about a tot of port and lemon?' asked Bert. 'That'll warm you through. Have one on me.'

'Ta! I don't mind if I do,' she replied.

Bert crossed to the bar and took her back a glass. 'Here you are, this'll cheer you up.' He put his own glass on the table and sat beside her. 'Are you living round this way?' he asked.

'Yes,' she said, 'just round the corner,'

'Do you live alone?'

'Yes. I've got a couple of rooms. Comfy and all that, but nothing special. Where do you live?'

Bert told her where he lived and how he came to live there, responding happily to a pleasant intimacy in her style of conversation and the solicitous manner in which she listened to all he had to say. In her crowded years she had learned that men like to do the talking – preferably about themselves – and with fog outside, business slack, a warm fire and a drink, she was content to let Bert make the running. Bert was a good runner. Seldom had he the chance to recount his life story to a pretty face prepared to listen to intricate details surrounding the cooking of food in Midland trains. Whether interested or not she gave every sign of being so and, far from interrupting, gave him every encouragement to talk, talk, talk until, even aided by the bitters and the port and lemon, he felt that his limit had been reached.

She finished the remains of her drink, stood up, pulled down her tight-fitting bodice, took a mirror from her muff, fluffed her hair and wished Bert good-night.

'Hang on,' he said, gulping down the remainder of his drink, 'I'm coming now.'

Together they walked through the swing doors, back into the mist.

'You know,' said Bert, 'it's a real pleasure to meet someone like you. You are different from the girls I usually meet in here. What's your name?'

2

'My friends call me Phyllis,' she said, 'but the bloke that christened me called me Emily Elizabeth Dimmock – though why I'm telling you, I don't know. Perhaps I've taken a fancy to you.'

'Well, Phyllis, look here. I've not got anything special to do tonight. What about having a bit of food? What do you say?'

'I'd like that very much.'

Bert brightened visibly. He pulled at his coat, extended his arm, and said with a knowing wink, 'Here, grab hold.'

There is no record of what occurred on that first meeting between Bert and Phyllis, but it was to be the first of many. Neither was deflected from their normal occupations; Bert Shaw still cooked his way along the rails, while Phyllis Dimmock persistently wandered off them. But they found that the friendship growing between them satisfied something which was missing from their lives. If Bert Shaw in his tiny kitchen car felt lonely, Phyllis Dimmock with her scores of transient beaux felt the need of more lasting companionship. She had trod a lonely road, which she sometimes trod again as she sat waiting for Bert to 'park' his train and take her out to dinner.

Born in 1879 to a working-class family at Walworth, she had trailed into the world after fourteen brothers and sisters; after a limited education and having reached an age sufficient to justify a small salary, she had entered employment in a straw-hat factory at Wellingborough, where her family now lived. She had little recollection of those days; she was too young to retain the details of the experience. But factory life was not her idea of work or amusement. Her needs were overlooked in the general demand which fifteen children made upon a working-class family. It was little different in the factory, where she was no more than a unit. One day cleaning straw, another day stitching hat bands, just one of the employees, and Emily Elizabeth Dimmock yearned for some outlet for her individuality.

Before long an advertisement for a domestic servant attracted Emily from Wellingborough. She applied and was accepted. Her new home was in East Finchley. At first, the change in her daily life maintained her interest. There were the holidays of one half-day during the week and every other Sunday. On those occasions she rode into the West End of London, to the shops, whose glamour and bright lights held a fatal fascination for her. She would flit around the London streets like a moth around a candle and with as much grace. Just out of her teens, she combined the bloom of youth with the attractiveness of maturity and, not unnaturally, her charms did not pass unnoticed by the young men whom she chanced to meet. They sought excitement, and Emily, in her new-found freedom, in the exhilaration of receiving personal and individual attention, was responsive to their every want. She was no longer 'little Emily' who, being the youngest, had to wait her turn (which never came). No longer was it a matter of checking in and checking out, just a number in the register of an employer. She compared it with the drudgery of washing dishes, washing floors, cleaning shoes and creeping off on her own for a half-day on Thursdays and every other Sunday. That was a mere existence; this was life as she conceived it – fun, excitement, money, glamour, pretty clothes and, above all, freedom. Emily substituted one old profession for another: handmaiden for courtesan. And with it she changed her name to Phyllis.

From there her story was little different from the story of all such girls. Soldiers, sailors, rich men, poor men, fat men, thin men, all kinds and all shapes paid tribute to her charms. She had her own little room and managed to purchase an old piano. Above all else she liked to please, and please she did. The postcards which she received from her erstwhile suitors bore testimony to that. Phyllis was not a young lady to be met and then forgotten. There was about her an air of sweetness. Pretty things appealed to her, and she collected all her postcards in an album, adding any other colourful postcard which caught her eye. She was easy to like and a favourite with all those who came in contact with her, male and female.

It will never now be known what attracted Phyllis to a friendship with Bert. She was not the scheming type and yet, had she schemed, she would have welcomed someone on whom she could rely for a more steady existence. Perhaps she sought the security of a home with opportunities for gay nights. For freedom or no freedom, life was not all honey. Somehow she had never attained the top grade of her chosen profession. There were grades of prostitutes, even in Euston Road, and she was fast becoming relegated to the lower ranks. But for the moment Bert was just a friend and, whilst his ambitions towards her were no more platonic than those of her more casual acquaintances, he treated her with greater respect than she was used to; it was both novel and pleasing to be treated as if you were really of importance to someone. Bert would have made an ideal guardian for her, but he was very engrossed in his trains and his cooking. He liked to take her out when his duty was finished, but he also had definite ideas about the person with whom he would settle down. He would not want a young lady who, although with him today, might be with three other fellows tomorrow.

As the months slipped by into 1906, Phyllis could be found parading the streets of London wc2. An occasional nod, a fleeting smile, a whispered, 'Good evening, duckie.' Then, a heavy footstep behind her and another conquest defeated by a policeman. Life was becoming a problem; the time had come to relinquish a little of her 'freedom' and the opportunity arrived in the early part of the New Year, when Phyllis met Johnnie Crabtree.

John William Crabtree was the lessee of premises known as No. 1 Bidborough Street. He liked to call it a guest house, but the visits of his guests were not of long duration – certainly not for as long as he was accustomed to stay as a guest. His last stay had been for a period of approximately three years. He terminated his tenancy when his landlord decided that he had outworn his welcome and sent him out on 'ticket of leave'. It is a way they had in His Majesty's prisons. It was Crabtree's boast that he had lived for fifty-five years and had only been in prison twice. His first mistake was when he allowed himself to be caught street-stealing. That this was a blow to his vanity there can be no doubt. He was a man, in the humble opinion of John William Crabtree, who was worthy of bigger things. So, when they let him out after that term of imprisonment, he turned his attention to stealing horses. At the end of his three years' penal servitude for that activity, he should, in strict progression, have given his attention to stealing elephants. Doubtless they were not a common sight in Camden Town and a man had to live. But Crabtree had 'the call of the flesh', and from horse flesh he turned to the human species, opening No. 1 Bidborough Street as a disorderly house.

It was a chance meeting which took Phyllis to Bidborough Street. For her it involved a disagreement with Bert, but its many advantages made it worthwhile. It could mean the end of perambulating the streets. It would then mean that the mountain would come to Mahomed. Phyllis moved in, complete with piano, piously hoping that her newest change was for the better.

Bidborough Street, Euston Road, Camden Town and the surrounding districts were not the places which exhibited London at its best. They were the homes of soft-feathered boas, of assumed respectability, where the public house did service both as a place of recreation and a landmark by which the visitor found his route. It was useless to direct a stranger to walk until he reached a public house; better direct him to walk until he found a building which was not. The public house, to the stranger, appeared to outnumber all other types of building, and of outstanding merit among them, both for the excellence of their beer and for the variety and vivacity of their company, were the Pindar of Wakefield, the Eagle, and the Rising Sun. Not far away was the Adam and Eve, so named, rumour had it, for its close connections with original sin. No. 1 Bidborough Street was not a famous address and John William Crabtree was no Rosa Lewis. Phyllis, installed in her new abode, became a constant visitor to all the local pubs. From these and the surrounding streets she sought her suitors, sometimes once, sometimes twice, and, given sufficient liquor and strength, sometimes thrice a night. From there she would take them to her room, and as she climbed the stairs to enter her place of work and rest, the ever-watchful eye of Crabtree would follow her with interest.

Not long ago he was assessing the business prospects of horses. Human material now afforded a much deeper and more engrossing study. There were few happenings in Bidborough

Street which escaped the attention of Crabtree. Life there was not one long round of fun, and it behoved the Landlord of No. 1 to endeavour to clothe his house with an air of respectability. As he often remarked, one of his tenants was a railway porter, 'a thorough torf, through and through, and I know a torf when I see one', and the expressed desire to maintain a respectable house afforded an excuse for the rapt attention with which he gazed upon the daily lives of his inmates.

But differences arise in the best-regulated families. In June 1906 Phyllis was to be seen taking a young man to her bed-sitting-room. He presented to Crabtree, viewing him from the darkness of his parlour, what would be described in Camden Town as a 'good catch'. He was about twenty-five to twenty-eight years of age, tall with artistic hands, high cheek bones and deep-set eyes. Not that this was the first time that Crabtree had seen the girl with him. He had been there during the previous month. 'Things are looking up,' remarked the landlord as he walked out to the street.

Outside, it began to rain and Crabtree had no business so pressing that it would justify his getting wet. Anything he had to do could well await a brighter day, so he returned to his house. As he entered the door he heard Phyllis calling his name. Slowly, he walked up to her room, and knocked at the door.

Inside the room the young man was sitting on the edge of the girl's bed. Phyllis, her hair down, was stretched out in the solitary armchair, naked except for a sheet which she had wrapped round her.

'Come in,' she called. Crabtree went into the room. 'Could you do my friend a favour?' she asked.

'Why not, Phyllis, if I can. What does 'e want done?'

'He's short of cash. He didn't bring his wallet with him.' She stretched out her hand in which she held a silver cigarette case, 'He'd like you to see what you can raise on this for him.'

Crabtree took the case. It was well turned, solid silver, with a monogram on it. Crabtree had not been street thief, horse thief and denizen of the underworld for fifty years for nothing. He screwed up his eyes. 'Whose is it?' he queried, opening it and shutting it with a professional air.

'It's mine,' said the young man. 'I would be deeply obliged if you could get me an advance of some sort on it. I am sorry to trouble you. I cannot imagine what made me leave my money at home.'

'Where did you get it?' Crabtree persisted. 'I 'ave to find out, you know. We want no trouble. If it's straight I can get money on it, but if it's not we shall have to be careful where we offer it. You understand me?'

'Oh yes, indeed! I fully understand,' replied the young man. 'As a matter of fact it was given to me by a friend of mine.'

'Oh no, that won't do,' said the questioner. 'They all say that. Give me def'nite details of where yer got it.' Then, as if suddenly visited by a revelation, 'By the way, aren't you the bloke who was here last month? You were having a bit of an argument with young Phyllis about some jewellery or something she was trying to get away from you and you flared up and called her a prostitute.... Christ Almighty.'

'Oh no!' interrupted Phyllis, glancing at her companion. 'That was nothin' to do with jewellery. That was nothin'. Come on, Crabby, be a pal. Raise him a bit of money on it.'

'Look here! You know as well as anyone that if this is hot they'll be on us like a ton of bricks.'

'Oh, please don't bother.' The young man walked towards Crabtree and took the case from him. 'I can manage.'

'All right!' said Phyllis, beginning to remove the sheet.

Crabtree moved to the door. 'Take my tip, you two, be careful where you leave that bit of metal.' He closed the door behind him, and stumbled down the stairs, mumbling as he went, 'Took me for a bleedin' twat.' Life in No. 1 Bidborough Street once again resumed its natural course, and the course of life in Bidborough Street was, if nothing else, natural.

Chapter II

Whether No. 1 Bidborough Street was too large or too small, too obscure or too well known, the redoubtable Crabtree decided to move. By the end of June 1906 he was installed in equally incommodious premises in Manchester Street. Perhaps he questioned the advisability of his move at a later date. It was for his conduct of the Manchester Street house that he was obliged again to accept the hospitality of His Majesty and, into the bargain, to complete his previous unfinished sentence.

Wise or unwise, he changed his address and with him went the greater part of the inmates of Bidborough Street, Phyllis among them. She was still on terms of the greatest intimacy with Bert. From their casual meeting a sincere friendship had developed, although it is to be doubted whether Bert was fully alive to all the activities in which his loved one was engaged. She was not increasing her status in the world. In most professions and walks of life the normal course is 'commence at the bottom and work to the top'. For the prostitute the reverse is the case, in every sense. Some scale the heights, but for many the passage of years finds them sliding to the depths. Phyllis was no exception. Soldiers and sailors on short leave were her speciality, she had reached a level sufficiently low to afford her little choice in whom she would or would not take home.

But, for all, she had retained her charm, and as Emily Lawrence, a one-time street walker, said, she was not yet one of the lowest types and was a very nice, respectable, clean and tidy girl. And to be very respectable, clean and tidy, even by the standards of the street walkers of Camden Town, was something.

Some, indeed, asserted that her charms had wrecked their lives. Crabtree recalled a suitor who caused him no end of trouble: a gentleman rejoicing in the nickname of Scottie. He recollected that this man had threatened her on many occasions, had accused her of ruining his life; on one occasion he had said that if his father and mother knew just what she had done it would break their hearts, and he intended to cut her throat and do for her. He was a singularly unpleasant fellow, and Crabtree, in the belief that he had knocked Phyllis about and on one occasion stolen her purse, endeavoured to keep him at a respectful distance.

Crabtree still kept a careful watch on his tenants. One evening in the summer of 1906, he chanced upon Phyllis plying her trade at Euston Station. Always a student of the world, he stopped to observe. But Crabtree was to be disappointed, for the girl had drawn a blank, and when she started towards Manchester Street, he naturally followed her.

She had not gone far before she was accosted by a man. He was young, about five feet, five inches tall, dressed in a dark suit and a wide-brimmed bowler hat. He slouched when he walked, and Crabtree, sensing an interesting performance, crept nearer. As he approached he was surprised to see that the stranger was the man he knew as Scottie. Phyllis talked to him in a torrent of words, and gave him some money. Crabtree's curiosity was aroused. Why, for God's sake, was she giving money to that scoundrel? If she had money to spare he knew where she could conveniently dispose of it. He was not, however, to learn what was afoot. Phyllis went on her way and Scottie on his; the investigation would have to wait a more propitious moment.

It was shortly after this that Phyllis went on a trip to Portsmouth. She had made the acquaintance of a sailor named Biddle, and had gone to the port with him. Crabtree regarded the whole matter as rather fatuous and compared it to taking coals to Newcastle, but it was hardly for him to interfere.

Phyllis had been away a few days when a young man called at Bidborough Street. He asked Crabtree where she had gone, and he told him as much as he thought it wise to divulge. The caller's face was familiar to Crabtree and yet he was not quite certain; having thought it over he came to the conclusion that it was probably the same man who had wanted him to pawn the cigarette case. 'Yes,' he said to himself, as amazed as before, 'I believe it's him. The bastard. Took me for a twat. Me! It's not believable!' He returned to his parlour and his easy chair, arranged himself with considerable care to ensure the most comfortable position, and closed his eyes, awaiting his afternoon sleep. He gave a groan of despair when he heard another knock at the outer door. He must have dozed, for whoever was at the door was knocking furiously by now.

'All right! All right! I'm comin'. Keep your 'air on.' He swung the door open. On the step, a horrible scowl dividing his countenance, stood Scottie.

'Where is she?'

''Oo the hell you talking about? And don't shout. I'm not deaf.'

'You know 'oo! Phyllis. Where is she? I've trailed up and down Euston all day. I can't find 'er.'

'She's not here. She's gone to Portsmouth.' Crabtree was thinking of his easy chair and his afternoon nap. He was in no mood to answer a string of questions.

'Portsmouth? Wot the 'ell's she gone there for? And by the way, 'oo's she gone with?'

''Ow the blazes d'you expect me to know? I expect she's got a contract from the Navy.'

'Gone to Portsmouth 'as she?' Out of his pocket Scottie drew a razor, and wrapped a handkerchief around the haft. He continued his diatribe – the razor waving furiously in the air – while Crabtree, who unusually had shaved that morning, retired to a safe distance.

'Gone to Portsmouth 'as she! I'll give 'er gone to Portsmouth. She's ruined my life. No one knows what I've suffered. No one. She's ruined me. I'll do 'er in. I'll cut 'er bloody throat for 'er. The bloody. . . .' Scottie raved and cursed while the razor beat the air in time with the imprecations.

It was really Crabtree's opportunity to enquire into the payment of the money which he had observed and which had so interested him. But Crabtree was a cautious man, and had a strong belief in remaining to the rear of the working end of a razor. Discretion is the better part of valour, and discretion, as it will, prevailed.

'Well!' said Crabtree. 'That's your affair. She'll be back and you can deal with 'er then. I've got work to do. Goo'day.' The door of the Manchester Street lodging closed.

The door opened again on the following Saturday to readmit Phyllis on her return. It was about 10.30 in the morning; she was tired and left word that she was going to sleep and did not wish to be disturbed. Crabtree sympathised. Leaving travel aside, he had no doubt she had every reason to be tired, and he went into the Euston Road to see the shops with his 'missus'. The 'missus' was a fruitful source of information to Crabtree. As they walked the dingy streets of Camden Town she would point the notorieties out to him.

Crabtree was trying to prognosticate in his silent thoughts the winner of the big race, shortly to be run. He paid little enough attention, but was always interested to learn who people were. One could never know when it might prove useful.

'Johnnie,' continued Mrs Crabtree, 'don't look round now, or 'e'll see yer looking, but that fellow there with the dark suit on, who just passed us on the uvver side of the road is a bloke who used to live with Phyllis.'

Crabtree turned and saw a dark suit disappearing into the distance. 'She's a proper girl, young Phyllis is, isn't she? But I'm a bit worried about this Scottie bloke. I'll have to have a talk with 'er about 'im. Sooner or later that bloke's going to do fer 'er, or me name's not John William Crabtree.'

On his return he wandered about the house, like the soothsayer waiting upon Caesar, until about eight o'clock. He decided that if he waited any longer he might not see Phyllis before she went out, and he climbed the stairs to her room. He expected to find her alone and was surprised to find that she already had a visitor.

'Oh. You're 'ere again?' he said in mock amazement. 'You don't waste any time, young feller, d'you? Blimey, you got 'ere before I could deliver your message. What d'you want this time? To pawn the Crown jewels or is it the Cohen-oor diamond.' A good-hearted grin spread over Crabtree's face. He always laughed heartily at his own jokes, in which others seldom divined the humour. The possessor of the heavy silver, monogrammed cigarette case contented himself by replying, 'Good evening.'

'Sit yourself down,' said Phyllis. 'Did you want to see me, dearie?'

'Well, Phyllis, as a matter of fact what I want to tell you is rather private like, and I think as it 'ad better wait till later.'

'It's quite all right. You can tell me now,' she added.

'No. I don't think so. I'll come back when you're free,' said Crabtree as the door closed after him.

Some days elapsed before Crabtree could find Phyllis alone. He went to her room when she was dressing for the evening.

'Now listen to me, young woman. You've got to be careful of this feller Scottie. I'm sure he'll set about you one day and do you no end of damage. He was fair raving mad when he came here. Of course, I stood none of his nonsense and soon put him in his place. But believe me, he's no bloke to trifle with.'

'Don't worry about me, Crabby. I can look after myself. Scottie gets very excited, but he's all froth and wind. D'you mind passing me that bodice?'

Crabtree reached for a white garment hanging over a chair, and shook his head. 'That's all very well. A bloke wot shouts and raves is one thing, but a bloke that argues with a razor is anuvver.'

Phyllis seemed unperturbed. 'Look, Crabby. D'you like these new sleeves? They're not as full as the usual leg o'mutton kind; and this little standing collar. Pretty, isn't it? Goes well with this black skirt. There, duckie, pass those camellias so as I can stick them in my waist.'

'Phyllis! You're paying no heed to wot I'm saying. If you don't want to take my advice that's all right. But don't say later on, as how I never warned you. When you're lying dead with your throat cut, don't come complaining that Crabtree didn't warn you.'

Phyllis was busily engaged in balancing a white straw hat with a large black band on the top of her bountiful hair, harpooning it with two long hat pins.

'All right, Crabby,' she said. 'I've heard what you've said, and I'll take care. Taking care's nothing new. It's as much part and parcel of my game as it is yours. If we didn't take care, where would we be?'

Together they walked down the stairs: Crabtree into his parlour to explain to his 'missus' what funny creatures women are, Phyllis to the familiar stroll along the lamp-lit streets of Camden Town, to the friendly atmosphere of the Pindar of Wakefield and the Rising Sun.

She pushed aside the swing doors, and entered the bar parlour. The Pindar of Wakefield was not her favourite rendezvous, but it made a change from the houses she normally frequented. The casual visitor would have discerned many features common to all the public houses in that vicinity. The smokiness of the atmosphere, the flickering lights, the drab and heavy appearance of the fittings, the sparse furniture, the hubbub of conversation, the mufflered men and the gaudily arrayed women who looked so much out of keeping with the dinginess of their surroundings. A place less suited to the purpose of arousing sexual passion was hard to imagine. But Camden Town, and least of all its public house, was not the spiritual home of the aesthete; it was the temporal rendezvous of the dejected; it was the appointed resort for the soldier or sailor, seeking a cheap quick thrill before hurrying back to his barracks or ship.

'Evening, Phyllis darlin'.' The speaker was Emily Lawrence; five years ago her purpose in the Pindar would indisputably have been to arrange terms for her nightly employment. It was her claim that she was now a reformed character. Since she married, she avowed, she had left 'the game'. Her only purpose in the Pindar these days was to enjoy 'a bit of recreation'. But reformed or not, she could hold her own in recounting past triumphs, and she was at home with the ladies of easy virtue, who shared her evenings in the public house.

'Good evening, Emily,' Phyllis walked across to the bar. In the higher circles of the West End her entrance would have passed unnoticed. Here, in Camden Town, she was alive to the attention which her arrival occasioned. The sailor on the left, with a scruffy little girl in red, closely followed the course of

14

her swaying bottom to the bar. The soldiers standing in the window nudged each other and looked in her direction. Their expressions were a mixture of admiration and 'Have I been rash in my choice tonight?' Their companions turned anxious and poisonous glances towards her. Phyllis feigned obliviousness to the stir she created. But she enjoyed it.

'What'll you have to drink, duck? A glass of bitter?'

'Yes, please,' she replied. 'Good evening, Joe, give me a half pint, will you?' Joe, the potman, produced the beer. He had produced the beer in this fashion for more years than he cared to remember. He had seen all the customers come and go, and the more he saw, the less he said. It was a wise policy for a potman to pursue in Camden Town.

'Been away, haven't you, darling? I've not seen you about this last few days.' Emily sensed scandal in every event; after all a few days' absence might be occasioned by a cold, but it might be something far more interesting. Why, it might involve an illegal operation!

'I've been to the seaside for a few days,' replied Phyllis.

'Oh yes, duckie, of course.' Emily looked hard at Phyllis, inwardly murmuring, 'You bloody liar.'

'Anyone been asking for me?'

'No, luv, not as I know of, but there's a dandy over there, right now, who you know.'

Phyllis turned in the direction which Emily indicated with her glass. A young man had just entered the bar. He was greeting the barman with a jovial 'good evening'; medium height, thin, he surveyed the customers from behind two deep-set eyes, which seemed to sparkle with an inward devilment.

As he scanned the bar his eyes fell upon Phyllis and he nodded his head in her direction.

Phyllis picked up her glass. 'I must go and speak to him. He's such a dear.'

'Who is he, duck? What's he doing here?' asked Emily.

'He's a young fellow I know. I'd take you over to him, but he lives with his parents and doesn't like to be seen talking to women.'

'Oh! That's all right. I understand. In any case I'm off now.'

15

As Phyllis crossed to the young man and began to talk to him, Emily followed every move. 'She's really a sweet kid, you know,' she said to the others, 'as nice a girl and as good a friend as any gal could want today. I've seen her with that young feller before. A real good-looker, isn't he? Well, girls, I'd better be orff. The ol' man'll want his supper warmed up. Good night.' Emily, reformed, married and pleased to be so, walked from the bar, with a wave to Phyllis as she passed.

Chapter III

For the next few months, day succeeded day with such mono-
tonous regularity that Phyllis decided to take an evening off. It
was seldom she took a holiday, but she had received a letter
from Bert. He seemed anxious to discuss some burning question with her. Poor old Bert, he was always worrying about
something. The way she lived; the things she lacked. Yes! Bert
was a good friend. Phyllis had made the room especially comfortable, cleaned it and dusted it. Now, she sat in her dressing-
gown, pasting into her album postcards which had taken her
fancy which she had seen in a small shop at the back of
Camden Town. She could never resist a pretty card, and these
were delightfully coloured and had such pleasing words on
them.

On the stair she heard Bert's footsteps and opened the door
to greet him.

'Hello, my little ray of sunshine,' he called. 'Am I late?'

'No, darling. I expected you about this time.' Bert kissed her
and sat himself in the armchair.

'I thought I'd have been here before this, but we ran a little
late today. I had a rotten day. They forgot to put enough
vegetables on at the other end, and I had the devil's own job
making do. One old boy only got one Brussels sprout but it was
as hard as blazes, and when he tried to cut it it rolled off his
plate on to the floor. There was bloody hell to pay,' Bert
drivelled on. He had picked up the album and was turning
over the pages. 'What have you been doing today, Phil?'

'Oh, nothing very exciting. Gladys came to see me this
morning. You remember her, don't you – Gladys Warren? I've

known her years. She was very kind to me once when I'd been turned out of me lodgings and she let me have one of her rooms. She's in service in Stoke Newington. She had to come this way for something and popped in to see me.'

'Poor darling,' said Bert, looking up from the album. 'You've had a rotten time of it. Chucked out of here, pushed into there. You've never really had a proper chance of living a normal life. As a matter of fact, Phyllis, that's one of the things I wanted to talk about.' Bert paused as if a little uncertain of his ground.

'To talk about, Bert? Why! It's not been so bad. I've had bad times, but I've had good ones as well. I've had plenty of fun. What do you want to talk about?'

Bert stood up; with his hands in his pockets he began to pace the room, 'Well, Phyllis, it's like this. I've been doing a bit of thinking lately. I get a lot of time to think travelling up and down like. And I feel that it's time I settled down.' Phyllis looked aghast.

'Settle down, Bert?' she echoed. 'Jesus! This isn't a proposal of marriage, is it?'

'Well, if you feel that way about it, there's no more to be said. I'll drop it. Come on, let's go out.' Bert was dissatisfied with his reception.

She walked across to him, pushed him into the armchair, fell on his lap and put her arm round him. Then she kissed him. 'Oh no, Bert darling, it's not that at all! But let's face it, what would you want with a no-good like me? A decent bloke like you deserves a decent clean-living girl. I may not talk about it, but I know what I've been and what I am. There are thousands of decent girls who'd jump at the chance of having you for a husband.'

A worried look came over his face. 'I know, Phil,' he said, 'you've got about a little more than's good for you and I don't like it. But I dunno: I feel you've never had a proper chance. I'm fond of you, Phyllis, real fond of you, and I am sure we could make a go of it.'

'But Bert,' she persisted, 'what would your mother say? You know only too well that she wouldn't like me at all. Just imagine taking me up to Northampton to introduce your wife to her. Just think of that, Bert.'

'I've thought it over and I know I'm right. I want you, Phyllis, and I've made up my mind. It's up to you now.'

Phyllis got up and walked across the room. This was the moment of which she had dreamed. Time and again she had tried to visualise the scene. Someone proposing marriage. A home – a measure of security. Time and again she had told herself she would jump at it, if it ever came her way. And time and again she had told herself that it was foolish to imagine such a thing. It was impossible. Now, here was that very thing happening, and here she was refusing. Dare she? Could she? Was it fair to dear old Bert? Dear old Bert with his soup tureens and cabbages, his steam trains and his worried look. Was it fair? And would it work? For all its dangers and insecurity 'the game' had, for her, much to commend it. She was a free agent, could do as she wished without responsibility for or to anyone. If she married Bert she could not cheat on him, but if she became restless and unhappy, what then? She turned towards him.

'Bert.' He looked up at her. 'Bert, I've got a proposition to make. If any ordinary girl said this you'd be shocked and perhaps upset. But I'm not an ordinary girl, Bert. Face facts. I'm a pro. I've lived in a brothel. Darling, if you're serious about this offer, I've an idea. I like you as well, dear, lots in fact, but because of that I cannot ruin your life. I'm prepared to come and live with you. No marriage yet. We'll try it out. If it works we'll get married. If it doesn't, well, Bert, we can say goodbye and no regrets. What d'you say?'

Bert did not know what to say. 'I don't like it, Phyllis. Here I am offering you a home, such as it is, and you're saying you'd rather have it without tying yourself to me. What can I say?'

'Bert, I know what's best. Do agree.'

'Look here, Phil. If I married you, I intended to have a condition. Not merely in my interest but yours as well. I can't make conditions under an arrangement like you suggest.'

She knew the answer before she asked, 'What's the condition, Bert?'

'The condition', he stammered, 'is that you would never go on the street again. That from the moment you married me, you would cut yourself off completely from all your past life and habits.'

'I knew that, Bert. I knew you would say that. And I would promise that just as much under my arrangement as under yours. I do promise that, Bert. Now will you agree?'

He walked towards the bed on which she was sitting and kissed her. 'You generally get your own way with me in the end, you little minx. All right, it's a deal. I pronounce you Mrs Bertram Shaw. From this moment, in the eyes of God at least, we are man and wife. Go on, get dressed. This calls for celebration.'

The New Year of 1907 had barely begun when 'Mr and Mrs Bert Shaw' were installed in Great (now Royal) College Street, Camden Town. The 'marital' home was nothing pretentious – two rooms in a dilapidated house – but it held a special significance for each of them. To Bert it became home in the sense that it was somewhere to return to after the work of the day. He no longer led a lonely existence, drawn to the public house for a drink and a chat; friendship was to be found waiting for him at home. Perhaps even more importantly, it meant that the girl for whom his affection was rapidly growing had been reclaimed from a life of debasement. To Phyllis it meant all this and escape. Escape from the uncertainties of a street walker's life; escape from fear of illness, too horrible to conceive. Escape from all this if, only if, she could resist the call of what she had left behind. For in all its degradation it cried to Phyllis to return. It required all her will-power not to succumb. Like a drug, constant indulgence had rendered it more difficult to stop.

For the present, she resisted the urge. She cooked Bert's breakfast and lunch, mended his socks and clothes, and generally tended his wants. Normally he left to catch his train in the mid-afternoon. Then Phyllis would tidy the two tiny rooms, put on her newest clothes and stroll into Camden Town to do her shopping. She made a special point of avoiding the public houses, unless Bert was with her; but sometimes, on the evenings when he was not on duty, they would visit one or other of her old haunts for a glass or two of beer or port and lemonade. Bert was more than kind to her. Within the limits of his small wage, he denied her nothing, and directed all his endeavours towards demonstrating that she had not made a bad bargain. That he had not made a bad one he was well satisfied. Travellers on the Midland trains might have noticed a spicier flavour to their food, an acceleration in the time of serving and a general improvement in the standard of their fare. Bert, approaching his work with a new zest, never tired of telling his co-workers that he must pack up his dishes quickly and 'get home, where the missus will be waiting'. Yes! It was pleasant to know that when you had opened the front door, and ascended those rickety stairs, someone was awaiting your return. Life these days was indeed good.

There were, of course, arguments, but never of a kind fatal to their happiness. On two or three occasions it came to Bert that Phyllis had been talking to young men in the neighbourhood. It was not that he was jealous, but he had sufficient intelligence to realise that, until some years had passed, contact with her old associates might adversely affect her resolve. He remonstrated with her.

'It isn't that I distrust you, darling. But you are better off without knowing those people.'

'They're my friends. I was only speaking to him. Do you expect me to walk past my friends and ignore them? Don't you talk to your friends?'

At times she behaved like a spoiled child. Bert took these differences philosophically, but as the months rolled by, he decided that a change of surroundings was indicated and they moved to St Paul's Road (now Agar Grove). This move was not wholly of Bert's design. In fact, as a result of complaints from a police constable who lived at the back in Great College Street, they had been asked to leave, although no reason was given for the request.

The new home was still in the Camden Town district. The same two small rooms, the same sticks of furniture with a few new pieces dexterously fitted into the general scheme of things, but St Paul's Road had a quieter atmosphere. It was secreted away from the fuss and bustle of the everyday life of the neighbourhood; traffic had ceased to use it; the dearth of public house and shops made it an undesirable route for the casual passer-by, and, with stronger reason, it held no attraction for the ladies of the streets. Its decaying houses, the dirty white curtains, the aspidistras dying in the windows; all tended to cloak St Paul's Road with the air of an old lady falling on hard days but struggling to retain her respectability. And No. 29, in which they made their home, appeared to be experiencing the greatest struggle of them all.

The landlady at No. 29 was Mrs Sarah Ann Stocks. She occupied the basement of the building, where she lived with her husband, an engine cleaner employed by the London and North Western Railway. She had lived there several years and had seen the old gas lamps in the Road superseded by the modern, cleaner electric lamps. Her tenants were her greatest worry. Her life was almost indistinguishable from those of the many landladies in the less salubrious quarters of London: it brought to all of them the self-same problems. The securing of tenants was a process of steering between Scylla and Charybdis, for the one lacked respectability and the other funds. In the final resort the Camden Town landlady was thrown back on the rent book. It was the badge of honesty, the hallmark of decency and the passport to society, before which the suspicions of the crustiest of lodging keepers dissolved. When 'Mr and Mrs B. Shaw' had suggested that they might become her tenants, her first question had been, 'And where's your rent book, duck?' Its production had sealed the bargain. Though the churches perish, marriage lines be irretrievably lost and free love be the order of the day, the magical words in the rent book were the protectors of the landlady's conscience. And in Bert's rent book, from his previous tenancy, were the words for all to see, 'Mr and Mrs B. Shaw'. The new tenancy was secure. Mrs Stocks was satisfied. She could rise at eight in the morning and retire at ten-thirty at night (eleven o'clock would be reserved for exceptional occasions) in the full knowledge that no couple so reliable as to have 'Mr and Mrs' in their rent book could do anything but uphold the unimpeachable integrity of No. 29 St Paul's Road.

The two rooms which Bert and Phyllis occupied were on the first floor of the building. The first room they designated the parlour. Here they put the chest of drawers, the armchair, the new chair and the sewing machine; on the little occasional table, in a place of honour, rested Phyllis's postcard album. In the window was the inevitable aspidistra, which seemed to be waiting only for the demise of the landlady before following her to its eternal rest. The second room was divided from the first by a folding door. That, they decided, would be the bedroom. Here they put the wash-stand, with the basin and jug, the towel-rack, a couple of chairs and, of course, Emily's most cherished possession – her piano. More furniture than this they did not possess. Although 'a handsome oak bedroom suite' could be purchased for £6 16s 0d, what they had suited their needs. As Bert so aptly said, a man could only sit on one chair, sleep in one bed and wash himself in one basin at a time, so why lumber up the place with more furniture? In any case, what more was to be expected for the princely sum of eight shillings a week? Could finer be found for such a rent? Phyllis agreed that for the amount of rent they were well served, but she sometimes had a heavy heart when, each Monday morning, she paid Mrs Stocks the eight shillings from the pound which Bert gave her as an allowance. That left her with only twelve shillings with which to provide not only food and other necessities, but her own requirements as well. However dangerous working the streets had been, there had been days when she had earned three times that amount in a single night. Respectability was a hard taskmaster.

Too hard, perhaps, for Phyllis. Excitement, both sexual and mental, money, changing company, bright colours and pretty objects were what attracted her, and these were the things which rendered the life of the streets as irresistible to her as a magnet to steel. Putting moral character aside, power to resist a strong desire is conditioned by the counter-attractions. There were few to appeal to Phyllis. When Bert was with her she was happy. But he left home almost every afternoon and did not return until the next morning. She was proud of her little home, inadequate as it might be, but this entailed a wealth of hard work to maintain it clean and tidy. Dusting, polishing, cleaning and not infrequent trips to the basement to the toil of the wash-house. Drudgery it was to her; hardly distinguishable from the drudgery she had known in domestic service in Finchley. Hardly different and without the luxury of an occasional day to herself. On the streets she had known many friends; today they were debarred her and in exchange no others were forthcoming. Bert was a dear, kind and gentle, but too gentle for a passionate woman such as she; he was a faithful guardian but an inadequate lover. Phyllis was slipping and found nothing to check her descent. Nothing excepting perhaps her word, solemnly given to Bert; her promise that she would never return to her old associations. Had she taken as her precept 'Be so true to thyself as thou be not false to others', she might have fashioned a different course. But the call of the flesh (as Crabtree would have agreed) outweighed the demands of the conscience and she looked for ways of taking up her profession where she had left it.

If there are tides which taken at the flood lead on to fortune, there are equally those which taken at that point lead man elsewhere. And woman too. For life at No. 29, with all its disadvantages in a virtuous life, possessed many advantages with virtue once forgotten. Bert was away from early afternoon until late the following morning; Mrs Stocks, the landlady, went to bed early and got up late; there was a comfortable room with a comfortable bed; Phyllis had the key to the front door; the street lights did not throw their light immediately on to the porch; everything indicated the ease with which integrity by day could be combined with self-indulgence by night. She had soon slipped back into her well-tried routine. With Bert steaming through the night along a Midland rail many miles away, chatting merrily about his 'missus' waiting at home with her postcard album, she would make her way to the public houses. Her arrival around eight o'clock each evening was again the common event, and when she felt assured that Mrs Stocks had retired for the night she would creep back to her room with the man of the moment. The wheel of fate had turned its full cycle.

To a woman of any other temperament the strain of living a dual existence would have been an ordeal; for Phyllis it added zest to the adventure. During the evening she could relax. The only poses she need assume were such as her calling dictated – the poses necessary to satisfy the whims of her diverse 'admirers'. By day, it was another story. The clothes which she was now able to purchase must be hidden from Bert's sight or accounted for; the hours of his absence woven into a mass of disarming falsehood; her tiredness, her conversation, her every thought and move required consideration or explanation. The months had lulled Bert into a sense of false security and the illusion that the bad old days were dead and gone.

The standard of her suitors had not improved, although she occasionally changed her ground in the hope that it might. Of late, she had shown a preference for the Eagle. As a public house, it had as much or as little to offer as the other houses, with perhaps one exception. In the bar was an automatic gramophone. Phyllis loved music; her ability to play the piano was a self-evident indication of that. The fifteenth child of a working family had small chance of becoming a pianist unless a love of music was already ingrained in her. The automatic gramophone was constantly at work while Phyllis was in the bar; a large proportion of the pennies it collected were placed there by her hand. She was listening to it on 6 September when Emily Lawrence, the reformed and married Emily, came into the Eagle bar.

The scene which greeted her was such as she encountered on her many visits to the bar 'for recreation'. The crowded bar room, the bartender working furiously; the manager drinking with a customer, walking the floor to see that all were satisfied; her good friend Emily Smith, with her elbow at the appropriate angle, and Phyllis talking to a 'male friend', as Phyllis usually did. She had the feeling she had seen the 'male friend' before. Wasn't it the young man with those delightful artistic hands? She was not quite sure. She walked towards Phyllis and bade her friend good-evening, as Emily Smith joined them. Emily Smith's original name had been Florence but for some reason best known to God and herself, she had acquired the name of Emily, which Phyllis had been at such pains to discard.

Phyllis and her friend moved to a table, by which were two empty chairs. They made no attempt to disguise their wish to be alone. As Emily Lawrence remarked to Sneeth, the brother-in-law of the licensee, who was serving behind the bar, they seemed very friendly. If Emily hoped to elicit some information from Sneeth by such an observation, she was to be disappointed. Sneeth was as reluctant to discuss the customers as was the potman at the Pindar of Wakefield. A noticeable hush fell upon their portion of the house.

There was no hush from Phyllis's table. She was busily engaged in talking and looking at some postcards. A young boy had entered the bar selling them and they were more than Phyllis could resist.

'Don't you think this is rather a nice one?' she asked her companion. 'I think I'll buy it.'

'Oh! I shouldn't buy that if I were you,' he replied.

'But I think it's pretty, and it'll go well with my collection. I've a fine collection now. All specially selected or sent to me by post. I like those best that come through the post. They seem more real that way. Yes, I think I'll have it.'

The young man put his hand into his coat pocket.

'No. You don't want that. It's not artistic and it lacks line. It's an ordinary cheap postcard which you could buy anywhere. You want something distinctive. I've got some cards on me which I bought in Bruges. Here, see if you like any of these.' He handed her several cards, which she carefully examined, expressing her views on each in turn. She came to one on which was depicted, in an oriental style, a mother holding her child. This she held under the light.

'Yes, I like this. It's very unusual and very nice indeed.'

'You may have it, if you like,' he said.

'Oh! May I really? Thanks a lot. But write something on it for me. I like my cards to have writing on and to have come through the post. Will you?'

He put the remainder of the cards back into his pocket and brought a sketching book and pencil from his right-hand pocket.

'Give it to me then,' he said, taking the card and resting it on the sketching book. 'How's this?' As he wrote – misspelling her name in the process – he read aloud, 'P-h-i-l-l-i-s darling. If it pleases you to meet me at 8.15 p.m. at the ...'. He paused while he sketched a sun rising over the horizon, the rays extending from the semi-circle and two eyes – one winking – a nose and part of a mouth. 'That's nice enough, isn't it? I think it's a nice idea. Now I'll finish it.' He continued writing, this time running ahead with his reading. 'Yours to a cinder. Robert Wood.'

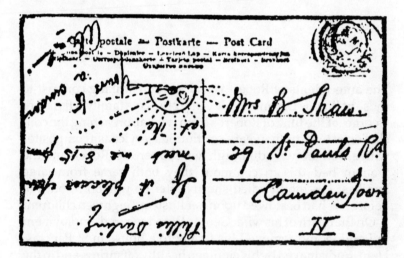

'No!' interrupted Phyllis. 'Don't sign your real name. If the ol' man gets hold of it he won't like it. Sign it "Alice" and address it Mrs B. Shaw, 29 St Paul's Road.'

He turned the card and did as he was bade.

'Now,' Phyllis persisted, 'you will post it to me, won't you?'

Robert Wood returned it to his pocket. 'Yes, I'll post it. Directly I get a stamp. I won't forget.'

Robert Wood's artistic fingers left no doubt in an observer's mind that, professionally or as an amateur, he was an artist. But he was not only an artist, he was an enigma. A far-flung net of fate had brought him to the Eagle on this night of 6 September 1907.

Chapter IV

The antecedents of Robert Wood were in striking contrast to those of Phyllis Dimmock. He came of a Scots family. His father George, at the time of Robert's birth, was approaching the conclusion of twenty-five years' continuous service as a compositor with a well-known Edinburgh newspaper. Yet Robert and the woman had this in common: they both came from large families. His mother died shortly after he was born, but not before she had bestowed upon her husband eighteen children.

On the death of his wife, George Wood secured employment in London and removed his family to a house in St Pancras. Here, undismayed by his eighteen healthy offspring, and in the knowledge that he was still commanding a good salary, George Wood married for the second time.

Meanwhile Robert had been put to school at the Thanet Church School, St Pancras. He was popular with both his fellow pupils and his teachers, and was generally regarded as being clever and sociable. He was now reaching an age, however, when he must fend for himself, and, having in the meanwhile won several school prizes, he entered the Australian Medical Students Club as an assistant steward. He had always been bent on sketching, and when this was known at the Club it was his frequent task to draw diagrams and illustrations from medical textbooks for the students and practitioners. During this time, some of his drawings were seen by an artist of note, who gave him advice and encouragement. Robert delighted in praise, and constant success in a limited sphere developed a conceit which, although not insufferable, was nonetheless undesirable.

In 1893 the Club at which he worked was obliged to close, and he set about finding fresh employment. He was engaged to design figures and patterns for glassware by a firm in Gray's Inn Road. His beginning was a modest one but by 1902, within a period of nine years, he had raised his status and his salary to that of a designer.

In that capacity he worked under William Moss, the principal designer. Both he and the remainder of the staff were greatly attached to Robert, and not unnaturally he bore an excellent character there. By the year 1904 he was twenty-six years of age. He possessed even then a character presenting a mass of contradictory traits. He had, so an observer related, 'long, delicate hands and tapering fingers; deep-set cavernous eyes and glistening eyeballs; high cheek bones; a broad mouth with twitching lips; a constant smile of sweetness and complete self-possession with a cheery and almost jovial manner, but withal there was a frequent lack of seemly seriousness, of becoming gravity, of conscious responsibility which was betides rounded off with a calm imperturbable air'. A complex being, indeed. He looked every bit the artist: his hair combed in an 'untidy' fashion, his sharp aquiline features, his clean but haphazard manner of dress, stamped him indelibly as a person of artistic tastes. But he had other tastes in which the physical outweighed the mental. As a baby, his left hand had been burned. This had left a scar on his third finger and his little finger was helpless and crooked. He was of a sensitive disposition and was always imagining this minor deformity to be an object of interest to those he met. Because of this a close and intimate companion might have observed that he often carried his left hand in his pocket. But only the close observer discerned it; the majority, contrary to his belief, noticed neither his injured hand nor his manner of carrying it.

To his family, his work fellows and his daily acquaintances, Robert Wood was a normal, affectionate, 'clean-living individual'. Many are the failings excused by the magic words 'artistic temperament', and if he possessed some trifling peculiarities they were overlooked on this score. Vanity, theatricality and verbosity were the signs of the artist in him, and were excused. Wood knew that he could, as ultimately he did, surprise them all, for the air of staid suburban respectability in which he enshrouded himself belied the way in which he spent his nights and the source from which he chose to draw his friends.

He liked to visit pubs where he might consort with the women there to ply their trade. Whether he went frequently or seldom, whether he went for the sexual or the social congress, whether he was actuated by sensuous or simply morbid interests was of no account. It reflected to his credit that he respected the feelings of his family. He was fully alive to the fact that had they known where he was they would have been horrified, and he spared no pains to withhold from them what even he regarded as his guilty secret.

This, when in September 1904 he met Ruby Young, was the intricate personality that was Robert Wood. It was a chance encounter in the Euston Road. The manner of their meeting remains wrapped in mystery, but anyone walking on the evening of that September day along that London street where many reputations have been made, and far more have been lost, could have seen them together: a young slim man of 'shabby genteel' appearance and a delicate-looking girl of not inconsiderable beauty. Ruby Young was an artist's model; the description served to cover a diversity of artistic indulgences. Her dark hair, blue eyes and pale face conjured to mind the paintings of the masters, her wistful attractive glances drew approval from the passers-by. She had started her way in life as a nurse, and had, according to some, paid for her attractions when she had been seduced by a doctor. She lived with her mother, but they were poor. Like most young girls, Ruby longed for pleasant times and lovely clothes, and since her first lapse had made many illicit liaisons with men of means. Someone had said, perhaps correctly but somewhat uncharitably, that she had been a prostitute frequenting Piccadilly Circus and Leicester Square: but it is likely that she was not so much an accomplished professional as an enthusiastic amateur. On this occasion, she and Wood walked together for some while and then made their way to the Rising Sun public house. There they sat, and drank, and talked, and found that they had a strong attraction for one another; it was the beginning of a close relationship, and within a few weeks they were together daily.

Ruby was living at that time in Liverpool Road, Islington, and Robert some distance away in King's Cross Road. Sometimes they would go to the theatre, sometimes they would content themselves with drinking in the public houses, but on most occasions they included in their programme a walk. The interests of both may have been better served had they – like the proverbial cat – kept on walking; but they did not, and within a short period of time intimacy had taken place between them.

By the beginning of 1905 Ruby had moved to Liverpool Street, King's Cross, and Wood was living not far away at Frederick Street, St Pancras, with his father and stepbrother James. Often Ruby would meet him when he left his work at Gray's Inn Road. She generally saw him at least twice a week and would often wait for him at the corner of the road. She was waiting for him one evening in particular. It was about half-past six, on a typical wintry London evening.

In the air the gathering mist was discernible; shops and offices were aglow with lights, beneath which industrious clerks scribbled with their pens; here and there, through the windows of half-lit rooms, the welcoming flickerings of flaming coal-fires seemed to beckon the waiting figure towards their snug warmth; workers scurried across the streets, their coats about their ears, mufflers protruding above their collars; a constant stream of traffic passed to and from the West End; the shrill cries of paper boys proclaimed the latest news; on the corner of the road a policeman vigorously beat his arms about his body in an effort to keep warm. London was pulsating with life and energy. The crisp winter air, with its misty smell, surrounded the little figure of the artist's model silhouetted against the seething picture which passed behind her. She was cold, bitterly cold, but she waited for Robert to arrive at any moment.

In the distance a familiar outline approached. It was Wood and with him was another person. Ruby walked towards them and saw that he was with a girl; as he had not seen her, she returned quickly to the street corner. A few minutes later he walked across to Ruby and kissed her.

'Who was the girl?' enquired Ruby.

'The girl? What girl do you mean?'

'You know very well, Bob, who I mean. The girl you were with just now.' At the best of times she was prone to jealousy. The thought that she had waited on a cold corner while her boy friend chatted to another young woman was more than her pride could stand.

'Oh! That girl, she's just a girl I know. I happened to meet her as I left the office.' His air of nonchalance was unconvincing. 'Why do you ask, darling?'

'Only that I've been hanging about here waiting for you. You might have thought of that before you stood yapping away with her. Who is she? What's her name?'

He paused as if he was considering which name could most conveniently be given. 'Oh! "Pansy". You don't know her.'

'No and I don't want to,' she replied, '"Pansy" eh? It was a girl I suppose?'

The bickering was becoming tedious to Wood. He did not wish his evening spoiled. He knew that if he replied in the same tone a first-class row would blow up, which might take days to put right. He tried other methods.

'Oh, come along, Ruby! Don't quarrel with me. The girl means nothing to me. I saw her and could hardly ignore her.' He put his arm around her shoulder. 'Come on, darling, forget about it.'

Ruby remained sullen. She would have preferred to continue her complaint, but she too did not wish to see the evening result in a definite breach, and he had given her the opportunity to retract. After all he was only speaking to the girl, but Wood knew so many girls and few of them displayed desirable features.

'All right,' she condescended, 'we shan't talk about it again, but I'd prefer that you left those girls to themselves.'

He ignored the final phrase. 'Now, sweetheart, where shall we go?' By this time they had walked the length of Gray's Inn Road, and had turned along Holborn. The shops were closed but the door of the public house on the corner of Chancery Lane stood invitingly open. They went in and had some drinks. In the warmth of the house the acerbity dissolved and was forgotten. They went to a theatre, then to a small restaurant in Soho, and it was late by the time they reached King's Cross. Ruby took her latchkey from her pocket and inserted it in the door, but it would not open.

'What's wrong, dear?' enquired Wood.

'I don't know,' she whispered in reply. 'I think I've been locked out.'

'Does that mean we can't get in at all?'

'Shush! Don't shout. I don't want to wake them at this time of night. No! I can't get in at all.'

She took the key from the door and began to creep towards the gate. Wood followed her, somewhat reluctantly.

'Where will you go then?' he asked.

'I don't know. I shall have to find somewhere. Where do you suggest?'

'Well!' he replied. 'The only place I can suggest is to come back with me.'

'What, to your home, with your father and brother there?'

'Oh, they wouldn't know! They sleep in the next room but it's divided by a folding door and there's furniture in front of it. Besides, they will be sound asleep by now, and you can leave before they get up in the morning.'

Sleeping with Wood was no novelty to Ruby, and it would overcome a difficult situation, however awkward it might be getting into and out of his home. They retraced their steps to St Pancras and crept into Wood's room; whispering and conversing by signs they undressed and crept into bed. The following morning, still whispering, they dressed again and Ruby crept away. In the adjoining room his father and stepbrother slept the sleep of the just, oblivious of the sin (as they would certainly have regarded it) being committed under their roof.

They remained on terms of the closest intimacy for the ensuing months. Wood went to work from eight in the morning until six-thirty at night. He enjoyed his work, and also his evenings with Ruby and his other 'lady' companions. Sometimes he would sit for hours sketching, while Ruby watched. He was very gifted with a pencil and his sense of caricature was remarkable. But his highly sexed condition or his morbid interests, whichever it might be, drew him to other liaisons, and inevitably they reached the ears of Ruby. In July the break came. She met him, as usual, coming from work and did not speak until they had walked some distance.

'Bob, I have been thinking a lot about us lately.'

'Really, darling, in what connection?'

'We cannot go on like this.'

He looked up.

'Cannot go on like what? I don't understand.'

'You understand quite all right, Bob. Only yesterday I heard that you've had that Pansy in your room every night for about a fortnight. Seeing me, leaving me and then going off with her.'

'How ridiculous. Where on earth did you get that story?' he asked with an air of indignant surprise.

'Never mind where I got it. I got it somewhere and some-where which convinces me of its truth. But then, Bob, it isn't only Pansy. You know you're always running off with those other women. I may be no virgin – but I draw the line at Camden Town standards. You call it jealousy, but I have other reasons. So long as you want their friendship you must do without mine. And since you will continue to seek their friendship, it's better we part.'

He remonstrated and denied, cajoled and persuaded, but all to no purpose. She was adamant; it was a decisive break in their relationship. True, it was shortly made up. But the rela-tionship had changed. It was Wood who was obliged to seek out Ruby's company, and the intimacy ceased. Whereas before they had met frequently, they now met not more than twice a fortnight. Wood directed all his energies to returning the relationship to its former intimacy, but to no purpose. Ruby had made up her mind; unless he was prepared to stand by her and her alone, he could find his amusement elsewhere.

The break between them was not an abrupt one. They drifted apart as if by a set plan, in clear and well-defined stages. The less he saw Ruby, the more he was in the company of others. His visits to public houses increased. The Rising Sun saw more of him than hitherto. It is difficult to say what were Ruby's feelings in the matter. With her own peculiar brand of loveliness she experienced no difficulty in finding male friends. Perhaps Piccadilly and Leicester Square saw more of her than before, at least until the New Year. For it was about that time that she moved to Earl's Court.

The move from King's Cross was another stage in their drift apart. When they had lived in adjoining neighbourhoods it was inevitable that they should occasionally meet. With Ruby many miles away the journey to see her was tedious, and where he had seen her twice a fortnight, they now met no more than once a fortnight.

Wood was as persistent as ever. He tried every way he knew to ingratiate himself again into the girl's good books. In the early part of the New Year his stepmother, the second Mrs Wood, died. She left him a ring, which he wore on his finger. Ruby admired it and he gave it to her. His was a perplexing mind. It could never be asserted with conviction what his intentions were at any given time. Almost from the beginning he had known of Ruby's nocturnal meanderings. This had not deterred him from discussing marriage. But that was long ago, and perhaps he gave the ring in the hope, unexpressed, that if more were read into his action than he intended, the results might justify the confusion. If this were so, his hopes were destined to be false. There were more fish in the sea than ever came out, and Ruby with her dark hair, blue eyes and attractive figure had the right kind of bait.

In August, he took his summer vacation and chose Brussels. While he was away he wrote cards to Ruby, but he found in the new surroundings other things and other persons to absorb his interest. In any case the cards reflected only the last faint glow of dying embers. Before he left England his relationship with Ruby was virtually a memory. Now they seldom met, and when they did it was by the merest accident.

A chance meeting brought them together again at the end of the month when he had returned home. He was in Cranbourn Street, wc, and met Ruby wandering along the road. They walked together for about half an hour, as they had much to talk about. They had not met for a considerable while and he had his holiday experiences to relate. It was part of the complexity of Wood that affectionate, charitable and lovable in his daily associations, he was almost the reverse in his relationships of the night. He had little use, it seemed, for female friendships unless they were satisfying his whims or needs of the moment.

The time might come when he would need Ruby, but meanwhile they parted, and left it to chance whether or not they would ever meet again.

His life at home was as normal as it had been when he had first set out to work many years before. His father was proud of the upright, straightforward and popular son. He returned his father's affection to the full, and his brother Charles could say of him 'he treated me better than a brother'. He was industrious and painstaking, solicitous and kind. He would get up every morning; go into his father's room for breakfast; leave for work at five minutes to eight, walk to his place of work, and arriving there about eight o'clock, be greeted by his fellow workers with obvious pleasure. Had his family or his friends been told that, at a certain hour the same evening, he would be consorting with prostitutes in a Camden Town public house, they would have laughed their informer to scorn. Yet Robert Wood had the charm of a Dr Jekyll. Could it be that within that kindly frame lurked the evil of a Mr Hyde?

So, on the evening of 6 September 1907 he was to be found in the Eagle, Camden Town, writing on a card, for a low-class lady of the streets. Drinking with her, joking with her, flirting with her; at home in her company and enjoying it. Moloch's hour was fast approaching.

Chapter V

At the turn of the century the foreigner found it difficult to comprehend the outlook of the average Briton. At heart, he was conservative: he abhorred basic change, and he saw no reason why he should depart from the habits of the past. In nothing was he more conservative than the matter of clothes. The Savoy's restaurants would only serve patrons in evening dress. When the Continental businessman changed into light clothes for the summer heat, the Briton, under sweltering sun, continued to don the clothes he wore throughout the winter. He might as a gesture have discarded his waistcoat, but, if he did, it was with reluctance.

So, on the day following his evening with Phyllis in the Rising Sun, Robert Wood was to be seen walking along Great College Street, Camden Town in his blue serge suit. Although it was September, London was experiencing a late summer and the day was one of the hottest of the year. The omnibuses, which passed along the road, contained more passengers on their top deck – open to the weather – than on the bottom deck, which was stuffy and uncomfortable. The horses, as they pulled their loads along the streets, moved as leisurely as their drivers would permit. The ladies, caring rather less for convention, were arrayed in thin, airy, summer frocks. The blazing sun had an enlivening effect and Camden Town, under its beneficent rays, had taken on a happier aspect: there seemed a little less grime, a little less tragedy, a little less penury, in its huddled streets.

As Robert Wood strolled, the evening was approaching, the sun dying and the neighbourhood beginning to resume its old familiar, crestfallen appearance. From behind he heard a voice bid him good-evening. He turned and saw Phyllis smiling at him.

'Hello,' he said, 'what are you doing here?'

'Oh! I came out for a walk. I got a bit fed up indoors.' They began to walk together. Their steps, as if directed by an invisible power, took them to the Eagle public house, which was close by. They called for drinks and sat talking.

'By the way,' said Phyllis, 'I didn't get that card which you said you'd send me. It was such a pretty card, and you did promise, didn't you?'

'Yes, I did. I'm sorry but I forgot about it. I'll send it to you today.'

'You really will? No pretending?'

'I really will,' he replied. They finished their refreshments, and Wood, who was going to see his brother, excused himself and hurried away.

Wood's brother Charles was a printer's reader, a married man who lived in Museum Street, Bloomsbury.

Robert spent a pleasant evening with Charles and his wife, and at about twelve o'clock wished them good-night and left. As he passed the British Museum he brought from his pocket the postcard, for which he had meanwhile obtained a stamp, and posted it in a pillar box which stood at the corner of the street. His promise fulfilled, he started for home and bed.

Bert Shaw crawled out of bed and emitted a mighty moan to the accompaniment of an equally mighty yawn. It was Sunday; since time immemorial a day of rest for the world's workers; luckier men were resting, but he was a railway servant and trains must run on Sundays as on all other days. He stretched himself, opened the shutters and walked to the wash-stand to wash and shave. Phyllis was already in the parlour. He put his shaving mug in the wash basin, and, in the process, Phyllis's ring and keeper which were lying on the side became drenched with water. He picked them up, dried them and examined them. He could not understand the point of having a keeper-ring to ensure the safety of the wedding ring if they were both to be left about the place.

'Phyllis,' he called to his 'wife', 'your rings are here. You'd better keep an eye on them, you know, with Mother coming here. If you lose them she might get curious.' Phyllis walked into the bedroom. It was foolish, she thought, to have left them there; he might be wondering why she had taken them off.

'Oh yes, darling!' she replied. 'I took them off when I was washing. Give them to me.' He handed them to her.

'Thank you, dear. When's your mother arriving?'

'She said she'd be here on Thursday. It's a long trip for the old girl, all the way from Northampton.'

'I'm very worried about it,' said Phyllis. 'Bert, d'you think she'll suspect anything? D'you think she'll like me?'

'Of course she will,' he reassured her. 'She'll like you all right. And you'll like her. She's a good old girl is the old lady.'

'I'll make the place look nice for when she gets here. I'll do my best with it anyhow. I'll wash all the clothes. You won't recognise it when you get in.'

They continued making their plans for the approaching visit, until the afternoon arrived and Bert set out for work. With him gone, Phyllis lay down to sleep, and in the evening, having dressed and painted, she set out on her nightly jaunt. It was a lucky one. She had walked only a short distance along the Euston Road when she saw a man coming slowly along the street. There was nothing unusual in that, but her professional eye detected some familiar signs. The way he looked at her, the constant turn of his head to see if anyone was watching, his half-grinning half-serious expression. If he was not a customer she would eat her hat, she thought, as she sauntered towards him and smiled; he smiled in return. She walked on for a short distance and looked back and saw he was still looking. It went according to precedent. It was as if the whole proceeding had been previously rehearsed. She retraced her steps and walked towards him. He waited grinning with a sheepish grin.

'Good evening, dearie,' she said. 'Are you looking for me?'

'Well,' he replied, 'I'm feeling a bit lonely like. I'm lookin' for someone.' It was unbelievable luck; a customer at this early hour. She took hold of his arm.

'What about coming along and having a drink then?'

'Yes, I think it's a good idea.' They started walking together, until they arrived at the Rising Sun, where they went inside. The usual crowded atmosphere greeted them, although it was early. But today was Sunday and with a holiday from work the customers could come as soon as they liked. They ordered their drinks and took them to a table in the corner of the room.

'What's your name?' he asked her.

'Phyllis,' she replied. 'What about you: what's yours? I don't suppose you'll tell me the right one. People never do, or what you do for a living for that matter. The last bloke I met here told me he was the Duke of Connaught. And when I asked him what his business was, he said, "Minding my own." It's usually a waste of time asking.'

'Oh, I dunno,' he answered. 'I haven't anything to hide. Me name's Robert. Believe it or not, Robert Percival Roberts. I'm a ship's cook. My ship was paid off last month and I've still got a little money left, so I thought I'd give myself a night out.' They sat drinking and conversing for some while until Phyllis detected he was getting restless.

'You don't mind waiting here for a while, dear,' she said to him, 'but my landlady doesn't get to bed until about ten. We can leave here shortly.' He nodded agreement and looked up at the clock.

'Hello, Frank,' he said to a man standing near their table. 'I didn't know you were coming in here tonight. Come over and have a drink with me.' The newcomer went across to sit with them, and Roberts introduced him as Frank Clarke, with whom he shared lodgings. He remained a short while and then left. It was almost eleven by then and they paid their dues and left the public house.

St Paul's Road was quiet, and No. 29, excepting for the thin rays of the street lights, was in darkness. Phyllis quietly inserted her key in the lock and opened the door. Roberts followed her inside. Softly they crept up the stairs, Phyllis leading the way. A pause while she unlocked the door of her room, and they went inside. She closed the shutters and put on the light. Roberts was wasting no time. He took twelve shillings from his pocket and put it on the chest of drawers. She called him into the bedroom. They began to undress. Phyllis put her clothes on the chair and lay naked on the bed. Bert had long since started his work; Phyllis was beginning hers.

Roberts left early the next morning. He was well satisfied; so satisfied, in fact, that he had arranged another meeting for the evening; so satisfied, indeed, that he was sitting in the Rising Sun at six o'clock waiting for Phyllis to arrive. By eight o'clock the bar was crowded, but he was not going to miss her, and the moment he saw her enter the bar he called her to his table. She sat down with him, and they became lost in the welter of customers drinking in the bar.

Whether she or Robert Wood arrived first was not clear, but about this time he was standing at the far end of the bar, where two familiar ladies were drinking by the counter. They were Mrs Emily Lawrence, the reformed Emily Lawrence, and her good friend, Mrs Smith. He looked round the bar but saw no sign of Phyllis.

'Will you have a drink with me?' he asked them.

'Thanks,' they replied as one, 'we don't mind if we do.' It was not unusual for this phrase to be chanted in unison. It occasioned no surprise and was a well-worn expression. The barman, Sneeth, handed out three bitters and silence fell upon the three, as the liquid began to disappear.

Mrs Smith paused and put her glass on the counter. 'You'd better not tell Phyllis that we've had a drink with you,' she said jokingly, 'she might be jealous.'

Wood smiled. 'Have you seen Phyllis today?' he asked. At this moment a slight gap appeared in the crowd and Phyllis, seeing Wood at the bar, stood up. 'Why, there she is: over there,' said Emily Lawrence, pointing across the bar. Phyllis came across and began to talk to him. He ordered a drink for her and she asked him for a penny, which she put into the automatic gramophone, and began to sway in time with its music.

'What are you going to do tonight?' asked Emily Lawrence. 'Staying here?'

'Oh no! I don't think so,' said Phyllis, looking at Wood. 'We're going to the Holborn Empire, aren't we? You did say tonight, didn't you?'

'As a matter of fact,' said the garrulous Emily Lawrence before he could reply, 'we're going to the theatre tonight too. We shall toddle along to the music hall for an hour or so, and by the way, Emily,' she added, turning to Mrs Smith, 'it's about time we were off. Well! Good night.'

The two pushed their way towards the door and left the automatic gramophone of the Rising Sun for the more melodious atmosphere of the music hall: they did not return until after the show, when they decided they must have one before going to bed. Phyllis and Wood were also there once again, while Roberts and another man were sitting in the opposite corner. A lot of business was still being done over the bar. They had not been there long, however, when they saw Phyllis and Wood go outside. They turned their attention to other matters, but a few minutes later Mrs Smith gave Emily Lawrence a nudge and an understanding wink; Phyllis had reappeared alone and was leaving the bar with Roberts.

When they arrived in Phyllis's room, Roberts, the ship's cook, made himself at home. He felt at home, having slept there the previous night. He had made up his mind that he would give her fourteen shillings as a mark of his appreciation. He was sitting in the armchair beginning to undress. Phyllis was taking off her bodice; she put her hand inside and produced a card.

'Mustn't lose this,' she said. 'I want it for my collection.'

'What is it? Looks like a card from here.'

'Yes, it is. From a boy I know. I collect cards. I keep them in an album. That's the album over there.' She walked to the chair and sat on the arm. 'See, this is it.'

Roberts took the card. It was a postcard and had been signed 'Alice'.

'Alice, eh?' he said. 'I thought you said a boy.'

'Oh! He signs that way. It's safer.'

She took the card from him, and he watched her put it in the left-hand top drawer of the chest in the sitting-room. She finished undressing; work had begun again.

By now his relationship with Phyllis had Roberts intrigued. It was not the sudden return to land, for he had left his ship a month ago; it was not the novelty of the experience, for he was no newcomer to this sort of thing. Perhaps it was solely the charm of his companion. Perhaps there were other reasons which were not apparent. Whatever it was, he made yet a further appointment and confided to Phyllis that he intended giving her sixteen shillings. She was dealing on a rising market. When the following day arrived, he took her to the theatre in addition and afterwards to the Rising Sun, to await the time when the landlady would be safely in bed. Shortly before closing time, Mrs Lawrence and Mrs Smith, from their usual vantage point, saw them leave for No. 29 St Paul's Road.

Meanwhile, Wood had met his brother in Theobald's Road, to go to his home for supper. They were rather concerned about their father. He was seventy years of age and the previous day had been obliged to leave his work because of an attack of gouty eczema. It was agreed that Charles should return with Wood to see his father, and, supper finished, they made their way to Frederick Street.

It was quiet in No. 29. Most of the residents were still asleep, or at least still in bed. But Mrs Lancaster was about. She was employed as a 'clerkess' and lodged with Mrs Stocks. She was on her way to the front door to find out who was knocking at this early hour. It was about a quarter to eight. She opened the door and found the postman waiting there, with two letters. They were both for Mrs B. Shaw, and she went to Phyllis's room, knocked twice, called out 'Two letters!' and slipped them under the door.

Phyllis got out of bed, ran across and picked them up.

'Two letters for me,' she said to Roberts as she sat naked by him on the bed. 'I wonder who they can be from.'

She opened them. 'This one's an advert – from a tailor'; she threw it towards him with a look of disgust. 'Ah, but this one's better. It's from one of my boy friends.' She got up from the bed and went to the drawer in which she had placed the postcard. She took it back to Roberts.

'Here, look at these two,' she said. 'Do you notice anything about them?' He took the postcard and the letter in his hands.

'Written by the same bloke, I should say.' He was not very interested, having other things on his mind. She took them from him; put the postcard back into the same drawer; the advertisement and the letter into one envelope, set fire to them with a match and put them in the grate. They slowly burned away. She watched them burning and then climbed back into the bed.

About half an hour later Roberts crept quietly from the house. Phyllis got out of bed, put on a nightdress and a dressing-gown and waited for Bert to return home. She washed, took her rings from the drawer of the chest and replaced them on her finger.

She did not go out again that day. When Bert returned she gave him some food, and went down to the wash-house in the basement to wash clothes.

'Where have you been?' Bert asked when she returned.

'I have been washing.'

'Washing what?'

'Clothes and curtains and things. I want it to look smart when your old lady arrives tomorrow. I've told you. I'll make such a difference you won't recognise it.' Bert grinned.

'Well, I'm on the Sheffield train again. I leave this afternoon, but I expect I shall be in by about 11.30 tomorrow. If the old girl comes before I get here, make her comfy.'

'I'm very nervous, Bert.'

'Nervous? You're a bloody funny girl. What d'you want to be nervous about? She won't eat you. She'll like you as much as you'll like her. And I know you will like her.'

He left to catch his train at 4.15, giving her a final word of reassurance before he went. When he had gone she went into the basement and collected the washing. She spent the rest of the afternoon tidying the room, and setting her hair in curling pins. She had to make a good show. Supposing his mother didn't approve? Women were such difficult people to deceive, particularly old ones. She was restless. This, or something else, was on her mind.

At a quarter to eight she was down in the basement again. She was dressed in a light-brown skirt and looked as attractive as ever, excepting that her hair was still in curling pins.

'Going out, Phyllis?' asked Mrs Stocks.

'Yes! I shall go down the road for a little while. It's very lonely up there all the time.'

'Yes, ducks! A good glass of bitter won't do you any harm.'

'No. That's what I feel,' she replied. She went up to her apartment and put on a short jacket. On the way down she passed Mr Stocks and said good-night to him. A few minutes afterwards they heard the door bang as she left the house.

About three-quarters of an hour later, Joseph Lambert, a bookseller from Charing Cross Road, was passing through Camden Town, and, feeling that he would like a drink, went into the Eagle. He was surprised to see a young man in there whom he knew, but had not seen for some time. He was standing by the bar talking to a smartly dressed young lady, who, he noticed, had her hair in curling pins.

'Hello, Wood,' he said, 'fancy seeing you. You are quite a stranger.' Robert Wood glanced towards him.

'Hello! Hello! Well I never!' he exclaimed. 'Come and have a drink.' He introduced Phyllis and called for a drink for Lambert.

Phyllis touched her hair gently with her hand as if in embarrassment.

'I hope you will excuse my dress as I have just run out,' she said.

'Yes! Yes!' Lambert assured her, and turning to Wood he said, 'Why, it must be months since I heard from you. Let me see: it was in February when I had a card from you and now it's. . . . What's the date?'

'The date? It's the 11th of September,' volunteered Wood.

'Yes, the 11th of September, that's seven months. Anyhow what brings you here?'

'Oh, I was this way on business,' Wood replied, as he moved along the bar to take the drinks from the barmaid. Lambert turned his conversation towards Phyllis.

'It is funny the way people pop up, isn't it? I haven't seen him for all those months and I happen to pop in when he's here.'

'Yes! It is funny,' she agreed, looking towards Robert. 'He's a nice boy, you know.'

'He is indeed,' said Lambert, as Wood returned with the drinks. They remained talking together for about ten minutes and then Lambert said he would have to be going.

'Well, Robert, it's nice to see you again. Let's hear from you soon.'

'Where can I get in touch with you?'

'I'm on the 'phone,' he replied.

'What's your number?' Lambert wrote his number on a piece of paper, handed it to Wood and with a parting 'Good evening' left the bar.

Thursday, 12 September 1907 was destined to be the hottest day of the year but one. Those who could perform their work in the early hours of the morning were indeed the luckiest. That was the time when Phyllis normally undertook her self-imposed duties. And two others at least in Camden Town hoped to have work to do before the multitude got up.

One of them was Robert MacCowan and he had to meet the other, Richard Coleman. They were out of work but hopeful this morning of getting new employment.

It was MacCowan's practice to walk from his home in Stanley Street, which he left at about twenty to or quarter to four, to Coleman's house near St Paul's Road. He was proceeding there when he heard some footsteps. They attracted his attention because they sounded as though someone had suddenly started walking from a standing position; yet he had not seen anyone as he passed.

He looked over his shoulder and saw a man leave the gate of a house and go towards King's Cross Road. He did not see his face but he noticed that he was wearing a dark overcoat with the collar turned up, and a hard bowler hat; besides a peculiar jerk of his right shoulder as he walked, he carried his left hand in his pocket.

It was a muggy, hazy morning and the man was soon out of sight. MacCowan continued on his way, dismissing the incident from his mind.

It was some hours before Camden Town was alive and the heat of the day began to assert itself, but shortly before noon an old lady climbed the steps of No. 29 and knocked at the door. It was opened by Mrs Stocks.

'Do Mr and Mrs B. Shaw live here, please?' asked the old lady.

'Yes, they live here,' replied the landlady. 'Would you be wanting to see them?'

'Yes, I do, if you don't mind. My name is Shaw and Bert Shaw is my son. They're expecting me.'

'Come in, will you,' invited Mrs Stocks. The old lady went inside. 'I don't know as how they was expecting you because his wife's still in bed. Of course he's not home yet, but he won't be long. You come and sit in my room and I'll go and tell 'er you're here.' The old lady remained in the basement, while Mrs Stocks went upstairs and called to Phyllis that her mother-in-law had arrived.

She had hardly returned to the basement when Bert returned home.

'Why are you sitting down here, Mother?' he asked in surprise. 'Why didn't you go upstairs with Phyllis?'

'Well, Bert, I haven't been here long, and your wife was asleep. This lady has told her and she'd have been down in a minute, but now you've arrived first.'

'Well! Come on up with me,' said Bert.

They went up to the room and Bert turned the handle of the door. It was locked. He knocked but got no answer.

'This is strange,' he said to his mother. 'She's always waiting for me when I come home. Hang on a moment while I get Mrs Stocks's key.' He ran downstairs and returned in a few minutes with both Mrs Stocks and the key.

'I didn't hear 'er go out,' said the landlady. 'I generally do, if she does like.'

Bert opened the door and went into the darkened room. 'Jesus!' he cried. 'Look at the state this place is in.' The others followed him into the room. It was indeed in a state. With one exception all the drawers had been pulled from the chest; their contents were scattered over the floor; a razor was lying on top of the chest, and another in the half-opened door of the sewing machine. Both belonged to Bert. The album which Phyllis treasured was lying open on the sewing machine. Bert walked to the folding doors, and pushed them. They would not move; they also were locked. He forced the doors and burst into the room. The shutters in the bedroom were closed, but a thin ray of light had pierced the joint. It shone into the room and was

47

sufficient to illuminate a heap of bedclothes on the bed. Bert opened the shutters, went to the bed and pulled back the clothes. His astonished gaze fell upon the nude body of Phyllis, lying with her right arm on the pillow, her throat cut almost from ear to ear.

Chapter VI

By the time that Detective Inspector Arthur Neil of the Criminal Investigation Department and Sergeant Page arrived at St Paul's Road, the Divisional Police Surgeon had almost completed his preliminary examination of the body.

'Well, Doctor,' enquired Neil, 'what do you make of it?' Dr Thompson looked up from his work.

'Hello, Neil,' he said. 'They've got you out, have they? What do I think of it? It's murder sure enough. Whoever cut this woman's throat did it with some degree of determination. He's almost severed the head, it's attached only by the muscles. A very sharp instrument to be sure. Come and have a look.'

The Inspector walked to the bed and stood beside the surgeon.

'Yes,' continued the doctor, 'a very sharp instrument. She would have been unable to cry out, once this job was started. I was surprised by the amount of blood. Look there. You see it has run in a pool towards the fireplace. Must have soaked right through the bedding.'

'How long d'you think she's been dead?' asked the Inspector.

'Difficult to say precisely. You see the body's quite cold and rigid. I should say seven or eight hours.'

'That would mean she died about five or six o'clock in the morning.'

'Yes, I should say about then, but I wouldn't like to state a definite time.'

'What's your opinion of it?' Divisional Surgeons were expected to know all the answers. 'What do you think occurred? Have you got any ideas on it, Doctor?'

'Of course it's impossible to be sure. But look at her position. She's lying on her side. Quite a normal position as if in sleep; her head's on the pillow, she has a peaceful and calm expression.' The doctor paused. 'It's rather strange that she should have her left hand bent behind her back in that fashion. There's nothing natural about that. Hmm, hmm – look at this cut on the sheet on her left side. It's cut the ticking of the bed as well. . . .'

'What does all that indicate?'

'I think that she was asleep. Her assailant was lying at her back between her and the wall; that's to say, he on the left of the bed, she on the right. He then put his hand lightly on her forehead, and grasped her hair. He lifted her head but when he took the sharp instrument across, he found her head was not high enough. It was then that he cut the bedding. He lifted her head a little higher and cut her throat, using considerable strength in doing so. I consider that, for some reason, the assailant must have drawn her left arm back into that unnatural position. I think those are fair inferences from the facts shown.'

'Yes, it sounds reasonable enough to me. What about blood, would the assailant have much on him?'

'No, not necessarily. He might get a little on his hands. But you see someone has been washing over there. There's water in that basin, some blood stains and a flannel petticoat in the water.'

The detective walked across to the basin.

'Any ideas as to the instrument? Could it be a razor?'

'Yes, I think it might. I saw two razors in there when I was looking round for an instrument before. Take them away and have them microscopically examined. They show no signs of blood to the naked eye.'

'Well! Thanks, Doc! I think I'll have a look round and then go down and have a chat with her old man.' Neil moved about the room taking notes of what he observed. After a short while he made his way to the basement where Bert, his mother and Mrs Stocks were consoling one another.

The Inspector walked into the parlour.

'Ah! Good afternoon. This is an unfortunate business. Are you her husband?'

Bert Shaw looked distinctly pale. 'Yes,' he said, 'that's me. Shaw's the name.'

'Well, I don't want to bother you more than I can help but I want to get a little information about her.'

'Shall I come outside?' asked Bert.

'Yes, if you prefer.'

Bert got up and walked to the door. 'I think it's better. They've had a rotten experience this morning,' he said. When he got into the hall, he was obviously greatly relieved to be out of the parlour. 'Look here, Inspector. I'm afraid she's not my wife. Not proper like. We'd been together some while but we had never been churched. That's my mother in there. She don't know. Nor does the landlady.'

'Oh! I see,' said the understanding Neil. 'Well, there's not a great deal I want to know at this stage.' Shaw was under suspicion. He was living with her, he was not married to her, and, if the doctor's hypothesis was correct, he had the greatest opportunity to commit the offence. He let Bert tell his story of how he found her dead.

'Did you find anything was missing?' he asked.

'Yes, there was. A silver curb chain, a metal watch, a box, a charm, a gold watch, a silver cigarette case – yes! a silver cigarette case. Let's see, anything else? Oh yes! a purse, a wedding ring and keeper and three keys.'

'Did they have any distinguishing marks?'

'No. I don't think so – only the cigarette case has a monogram on it.'

'Well! Thanks, Shaw. I'll let you know if I need you again. I expect I shall want to see you later.'

'Okay, Mr Neil. I'll be about whenever you need me.'

The qualities which go to make a successful police officer are as diverse as they are rare, and not least among them are intelligent appreciation of facts, hard work and a knowledge of the neighbourhood in which it is necessary to operate. These were the factors which were to keep Detective Inspector Neil engaged throughout the ensuing nights.

Before many hours had passed, and while the *Lusitania* was

breaking the record for the Atlantic crossing, he had unearthed the details of Phyllis's daily existence. All the exploits so carefully and skilfully withheld by her from Bert were disclosed to the searching gaze of the police. It was a short cry from these discoveries to securing information about Roberts.

So, half an hour after midnight, Inspector Neil and his assistant presented themselves at Roberts's lodgings. The visit was not entirely unexpected. He had learned of the murder that afternoon, when he was in the Rising Sun. Already it had become the gossip of the neighbourhood; it was soon to become the sensation of the country.

Roberts, the ship's cook, was anxious to assist; too anxious to assist. He gave descriptions of the man with whom he had seen Phyllis; he described his own amorous adventures with the dead girl and he engaged in ornate and elaborate recitations of the contents of the postcard and letter which he had seen. A postcard and a letter. The police officers were interested. Where had he last seen them? He described how the letter had been burned in the grate and the postcard had been replaced in the top left-hand drawer of the chest in the sitting-room. That was sufficient for a day; they decided to get some rest and commence a search for the card and burned paper at first light the following morning.

While the citizens of London were reading in their morning papers of the horrible surprise which awaited Mr Bert Shaw on his return from work, Detective Sergeant Osborne was searching Shaw's rooms at St Paul's Road; while the citizens' bacon and eggs were congealing on their plates, their coffee and hot rolls becoming cold, while their fond wives nagged them not to read at breakfast and, having heard what they were reading, sat themselves down to read it with them; while, in short, the newspaper-reading public were awakening to the realisation that a new murder sensation was on their hands, Sergeant Osborne had found the charred paper and was searching the drawers for the postcard.

He lifted the clothes from the top drawers, lifted the newspaper doing service as a liner, but could find no trace of a postcard. Three rings were found in the drawer, and those and a photograph of Phyllis wearing a sailor hat were taken by the police, but it was assumed that the postcard had gone the way of the burned letter. They did not know Phyllis; was she likely to have burned a precious postcard? As the police investigations proceeded, the field of suspects was gradually reduced; one by one, the possible assailants were eliminated. Bert Shaw appeared to have a cast-iron alibi; he was in Sheffield when the murder occurred; that is assuming, of course, that the medical opinion as to the time of death was the correct one. The women, such as the landlady, appeared to have neither the strength to have dealt with the girl's throat in the manner indicated, nor the motive nor special opportunity. But the mere presence of alibis might be misleading. By this time alibis were flying fast and furiously. Roberts, the ship's cook, produced his friend Frank Clarke to confirm that he was in the Rising Sun throughout the Wednesday night and that they walked back to their lodgings together after closing time. They both said that their landlady had admitted them to the lodgings. Others were seeking alibis with equal fervour.

Perhaps the last person with intimate knowledge of the actors in the drama to whom news of the murder seeped was Crabtree. He was playing the guest again; the police had terminated his lease of another disorderly house in King's Cross Road and put him into prison again. It did not increase the admiration in which Mr Crabtree might be disposed to hold the police. When they enticed him from his cell, told him of the murder and began to question him, he felt the acme of injustice had been reached. He had a cast-iron alibi. Short of the Indian rope trick or walking miraculously through prison walls, he was well and truly incarcerated at the time the murder was committed. But although the English police might be the pride of the British and 'wonderful men' to the Americans, in the eyes of Crabtree the whole force had been raised only to pester and tantalise Crabtree. He did not put it beyond them to 'pin' the crime on him, and he felt anything but happy. He told them what he knew of Phyllis's behaviour in the time he knew her, of the threats of Scottie and his waving razor, of the move to live with Bert, and of her general manner of late. He told them all he knew of the matters upon which they questioned him; but he told them no more. As he was forever relating, he was not one to assist the police at any time, and having pushed him as far along the road of recollection as appeared possible, they bundled him into his cell again and banged the door.

The days were passing and progress was slow. In truth it was hard to assert that progress had been made at all. Scottie was nowhere to be found, although another gentleman mentioned by Crabtree as a 'possible' and known as Scotch Bob was traced; but he produced an alibi which showed him to have been in Scotland on the Wednesday.

Hopes of effecting an arrest were receding when, some three weeks after the murder, Bert Shaw was moving from his rooms to other quarters. While emptying the chest in the sitting-room he threw the newspaper lining on to the floor and the Rising Sun postcard fell from between the pages. The police immediately caused facsimiles to be produced in many daily newspapers. And on Sunday, 29 September, the *News of the World* reproduced it with the caption 'Can you recognise this?' To anyone who could give information enabling the writing to be identified they offered £100. To all intents and purposes it elicited no response, and this was not the only occasion on which the assistance of the public had been sought without result. Mrs Lawrence and Mrs Smith, to say nothing of several other persons, had told the police about the young gentleman with whom Phyllis had so often been seen, but, so far, he had not returned to the Rising Sun and no one knew where, or who, he was. By an admixture of the information received, the police had secured some features which were common to all the descriptions and had, through the medium of the daily papers, asked the public to trace a man 'About 30 years of age. 5 feet 7 inches in height. Has a long thin blotchy face and sunken eyes. He was wearing a blue serge suit, a bowler hat with a somewhat high crown, a double collar and a dark tie. He is a man of good education and shabby genteel appearance.'

Even MacCowan had not delayed to provide a description. Within a day or two of the discovery of the body he had been to the police and told them of the man he had seen in St Paul's Road while on his way to secure employment. He had described the peculiarity of the man's walk, the jerk of his shoulders and his left hand in his pocket, which had so much attracted his attention. It was all to no avail. The shabby gen-teel man, in spite of the murder being the talk of London, could well be jerking his way round the London streets, his hand thrust into his pocket, without anyone so much as noticing him.

Phyllis Dimmock had been laid to rest; the Central London coroner had opened the inquest; time was marching on; and the daily newspapers, as only daily newspapers can, were announcing that an arrest was imminent. The newspapers were obviously better informed than the police; the imminence of an arrest presupposed that the murderer was known. The police would have paid a great deal for his name.

The Camden Town murder was no less the topic of discussion at the drawing office in Gray's Inn Road than elsewhere. Some were interested in it, to the point of wishing to discuss it, such as William Moss, the principal designer; others preferred to cut discussion short, such as Robert Wood. So, when on 13 September the papers announced the grisly happenings in St Paul's Road, Moss had remarked to Wood that he saw that another of those unfortunate women had been done to death. It was not a profound remark, nor was it intended to be. It was just one of those remarks which go to make conversation. But Wood was in no mood for conversation and, having observed that he was not surprised at that kind of thing happening, as they never knew whom they were taking home, he was con-tent to allow the conversation to lapse.

If Wood was outwardly uninterested in the exciting story being passed from person to person throughout the length and breadth of the country, inwardly he paid far more heed to it than his demeanour indicated. The telephone number which Mr Lambert had given him in the Eagle was put to good pur-pose and on 20 September Lambert received a telephone call.

'Hello. This is Lambert. Who are you?'

'This is Wood this end – Robert Wood.'

'Oh hello, Wood. How are you? What can I do for you?'

'Well, it's like this. Have you heard about the Camden Town affair?'

'Yes, Wood, I have. What about it?'

'Well, it's about that. Mr Moss has mentioned it to me and I've been thinking about it. Of course, I can clear myself. . . .'

'Look here, Wood, I'd rather not discuss this over the telephone. You'd better come and see me.'

'Yes,' replied Wood, 'I'll probably come over tomorrow.' They terminated the call, but a few minutes afterwards, Wood telephoned again and, having enquired what time Lambert closed his office, said he would be over during the evening.

On that same Friday, 20 September, Ruby Young received a telegram. The contents surprised her: 'Meet me 6-30, Phit-Eesi's, tonight, – Bob'. She had not heard from Wood since their chance meeting the previous month after his return from the Continent.

Ruby went to the bootshop in Southampton Row and met him. They went to a tea shop, and she was so curious she hardly let him sit down before she asked him why he had sent the telegram.

'The reason's this, darling. If any questions are put to you, will you say that you always saw me on Mondays and Wednesdays?'

Ruby was perplexed. 'But why, Bob? Why should I say that and who will ask questions?'

'The reason does not matter for the moment. Will you say it?'

'Well,' she hesitated. 'Yes, I suppose so. If you want me to.' His tone was so final; she was intrigued to know his reason, but it was obvious he had no intention of disclosing it. They finished tea, and Wood made ready to go.

'I've got to go to Charing Cross Road; will you walk that way with me?'

'Yes,' she said, still very curious, 'if you like. What are you going to do there?'

'Oh! I'm only going to Westall's the booksellers. Mr Lambert works there. I'm going to see him.'

'All right then, I'm ready.'

'By the way, Ruby,' he added, 'I'm going to see that show *Miss Hook of Holland* at the Prince of Wales Theatre next

Monday. They say it's very good. I'd like you to come with me – will you?'

Her curiosity was greater than ever. What had happened to him? She sees nothing of him, then he sends a telegram; when she meets him, it is only to ask her to say they always spent certain days together; no sooner has she drunk her tea than he's off again, and then, after all this time, he invites her to go the theatre with him.

Her mind was in a turmoil as she replied, 'Yes, Bob, I'd like to.'

They walked to Charing Cross Road, and he left her to make his way to Mr Lambert. The preliminaries completed he got down to serious discussion.

'... so the upshot of it all is this. I want to avoid the publicity of the affair. If Mr Moss says anything to you about it, you might tell him we met and had a drink, but leave the girl out.'

'That will be all right,' said Lambert.

'Good then,' replied Wood, 'that's settled. So far as you are concerned you know nothing about it. We met – had a drink, but you know nothing more.' Another bargain was sealed and, likewise, another pair of lips.

Wood had no intention of letting Ruby forget. On the following Monday she received a card: 'Sweetheart, if it is convenient for you, will you meet me as before, Phit-Eesi's at 6-30 and we will have tea together, and then go the theatre, which I hope will be a little ray of sunshine in your life. Good-bye.' She complied and they went to the theatre, but he made no mention of his previous discussion beyond reminding her before he left, 'Mondays and Wednesdays, don't forget.'

Ruby was still puzzled. She could get no further information from Wood, not even about his sudden disposition to renew their old relationship after weeks of absence. But Ruby read the *News of the World*, which was not surprising, and on 20 September her eye was scanning that worthy journal when she saw some arresting words: 'Can you recognise this?' To Ruby the singular part was that she could and did. The curtain was lifting for her. She cut the facsimile postcard from the paper, wrote a letter to Wood, and put it on the table, until such time as she could go out and post it.

That evening, before she had sent the letter, she received a visitor. She answered the door and to her surprise found Wood waiting on the step.

'What on earth brings you here, Bob?' He was obviously agitated.

'Ruby,' he said, 'I'm in trouble.'

Ruby took the envelope from the table, opened it and handed him the cutting. 'Yes, I know,' she replied. 'This is your handwriting.'

'Ruby, have patience and I will tell you all.' He took a cigarette from his case and sat down in an armchair.

'It all began on a Friday. I was walking along Euston Road with a friend and went into the Rising Sun for a drink. While I was there a girl came up and asked me for a penny for the electric gramophone....' He went on with his story from there, about the boy with the postcards, how he had written it at her request, how he had met her the next day, when she had reminded him of the card, and how he had sent it off.

Ruby was listening intently. He went on, 'The following Monday evening, I was going along the Euston Road, and looked into the Rising Sun. I saw one of the girl's women friends. She said, "Phyllis has not seen you yet. She's in the corner over there." Her friend signalled to her and she came running over. We had a drink and then she said, "I'll be back in a moment," and went outside. She was a long while, so I followed her out. As I was crossing the road I saw her talking to a lame man. She called out to me, "What about my drink?" I said, "I thought you weren't coming back." She turned to the lame man and said, "I'll see you when the house closes," and we went back into the pub and had another drink. I walked up Euston Road with her later, and then left her. That was the last time I saw her. I was with my brother Charles on Tuesday, and on Wednesday I was out walking alone....'

Ruby was waiting for him to continue, but he said no more.

'Hmm!' she finally said. 'That's a pretty kettle of fish, but surely the best thing to do is tell the whole story to Scotland Yard. If you told them all you've told me, you'd be quite free.'

'No, Ruby!' he replied. 'I can't do that. I have no one to prove where I was on Wednesday. Several people have noticed the writing. Mr Moss said that he'd seen it and that it was obvious that an artist had written it.'

'What did you say?'

'Oh! I said I wouldn't be surprised if he had. Then Tinkham recognised that it was my handwriting.'

'Who's he? I don't think I know him.'

'Yes, you do, he's the foreman. He said he'd recognised it. I told him it was my writing and told him everything I have told you.'

'What did he say?' she asked.

'Well, I told him about Dad. I told him that he had gouty eczema and that if he got to know I had been with that woman and got mixed up with it, it would have dire results. He said he would say nothing about it.'

She paused for a while and then said slowly, 'And what do you want me to do about it, Bob?'

'I want you to say that you were with me on Wednesday. You know how ill Dad is. I cannot risk what will happen if he gets to know.'

'But where were you on Wednesday?'

'Oh, I was nowhere in particular. Just walking about; nowhere in particular at all. Please, Ruby. Do this for me.'

'It's all very fine, but it might get me into trouble. Suppose they find out that I was not with you, what then?'

'You need not fear that, Ruby darling. Your word and mine would stand against the world.'

'Well, I don't know if I'm doing right, but – I'll say it. Still, we'd better work out where we'll say we'd been, in case someone asks.'

'Yes, we'd better do that.'

'Well, we'll say I met you at Phit-Eesi's and had tea. After tea we walked down Kingsway, along the Strand and straight along to Hyde Park Corner; from there we went through the Park out to Brompton Oratory. We would be there about 10.30 and from there, we parted, and went home. That would get you back just before midnight.'

He sighed with obvious relief. 'That's fine, sweetheart! We'd better say that you met me at 6.30.' They went through the details again until they had them word perfect.

'Everyone has been very kind to me. Even my brother Charles,' he told her.

'Why! Does he know all about it?' she asked.

'Yes. I've just come from him. I told him all I've told you and we decided not to go to the police yet. But we've written a letter and sent it to an accommodation address. If anything is said later as to why we didn't go to the police, we can produce that. Here's a copy, would you like to see it?'

She took the letter from him and opened it. It was headed from Museum Street, dated 29 September 1907 and read:

We, the undersigned, make this statement and place it in the charge of the poste restante at St Martin's le Grand in order to safeguard our good faith in the matter should our course of action be impeached. We, the first two signatories, are aware from his own full avowal that the postcard published in the newspapers of September 27th and 28th, by desire of the police in order to obtain information in the Camden Town Murder Case, is in the handwriting of, and was written by, Robert Wood, of 12 Frederick Street. We jointly are anxious to help the police in every way possible: but we are also anxious to avoid the publicity and personal trouble occasioned by an immediate communication. Having regard to the non-reliability of newspaper reports, theories and comments, and being quite satisfied of Robert Wood's bona fides and that his contribution to the matter can aid but little, we consider it wise to await the results produced at the adjourned inquest on September 29th, and while trusting that the intervention of Robert Wood may thereby be unnecessary, at the same time we determine, should no satisfaction arise from the inquest, to make the avowal of Robert Wood without delay. Signed. Charles Carlyle Wood, Bessie M. Wood, Robert Wood.

Ruby finished reading it and handed it back to him.

'Yes, Bob, I think that's a good idea. I should hate my name to get into the papers. My mother would be hurt so.'

'I know how you feel, Ruby. If your name gets besmirched in any way I will marry you – if I get free.' Wood felt happier than he had felt for some days.

Ruby was not happy; she was drifting in a sea of uncertainty; she was torn between the fear of implication in the gruesome business of a murder trial and the reluctance to go back on her word. She met Wood on occasions. They spoke very little about the subject, but he allowed no opportunity to pass without imploring her to be true, and to say she was with him on the Wednesday. It was playing on her nerves, and on one occasion when he repeated his entreaty she told him so, in no uncertain fashion.

But Ruby was a woman, and a woman not merely with a secret, but with a secret which might involve her. She met a friend, a good friend who would only advise her for the best. It could not possibly hurt to tell him just a little about it, no names, no details, just the general outline, just the barest facts and get his advice. The more she thought about it, the better the idea appealed to her, and the more her resistance weakened. She had led a life of weakening resistances. She had learned to weaken her resistance with grace and charm, and she finally gave way. She told the friend. He told a representative of the *Weekly Despatch*; the representative of the *Weekly Despatch* told the police and when the seriousness of the position had been explained to Ruby she met Inspector Neil at Piccadilly Circus tube station.

It was arranged that Neil would meet Ruby later in the day at Gray's Inn Road, when she would point out Wood to him. Ruby was sad about what she had done, but she had been assured that it was the only thing to do and that she should never have agreed to withhold information from the police. That all would turn out well for Robert she had no doubt.

At six o'clock that evening, she was waiting at Gray's Inn Road – the self-same corner where she had so often waited for Wood to leave work. Then she had been waiting as a lover, now she waited as a decoy. At 6.15 Wood came from the office and started along the road. She walked up to him.

'Hello, Ruby darling!' he said. 'I didn't expect to see you here today.'

'No!' she replied. 'I know you didn't.' They began to walk along the road towards Holborn. Wood was looking back at a man who was following them.

'Ruby,' he said, 'you see that man over there; I believe he's a detective.'

'I should take no notice,' she replied.

He was not left long in doubt. A voice behind him called, 'Mr Wood!' He stopped and turned. 'I am a police inspector and I wish to speak to you.'

'Certainly,' he replied.

'I do not wish this lady to hear. Kindly step this way, will you?' Wood moved away with the Inspector, and Neil continued, 'I have been making certain enquiries as to the murder of Emily Elizabeth Dimmock at 29 St Paul's Road, Camden Town on the night of 11 September, and some postcards have been found which were sent to her by a man with whom she was acquainted. From my enquiries I have reason to believe that they were written to her by you and that you knew her as "Phyllis".'

'Yes,' he replied, 'that's quite right. There's no mystery about the card. I only wrote one of them. The one with the "Rising Sun" on it. I know nothing about the others.'

'You had better come with me,' said the Inspector. 'We can't discuss the matter here. I shall have to detain you pending enquiries as to your movements on the night of 11 September, which was the night of the murder. I have reason to believe that you know something about it.'

'Very well,' said Wood, 'you'll allow me to wish my young lady goodbye before I go.' He went towards Ruby and spoke to her. As the police hailed a passing taxi, and directed Wood into it, she was crying – whether it was remorse or pity was not to be deduced, but it served to delude Wood into the belief that she was innocent of all complicity in his detention. He entered the taxi, but stopped on the step and said to Ruby, 'Goodbye, dear; don't worry. I have to go with these gentlemen. If England wants me she must have me. Don't cry, but be true.'

The taxi jolted its way towards Highgate. While Neil and Sergeant Ball showed a disinclination to discuss the affair until they reached the police station, Wood was anxious to talk. He kept saying that he had made no secret of the card and that he wanted to make a statement. They told him to wait until they got to the station.

When they arrived and the usual formalities had been gone through, they sat at a table, Wood on one side, the Inspector on the other.

'Now, Wood,' said the Inspector, 'I have to caution you. You do not have to make a statement, although you may do so if you wish, but whatever you say will be taken down in writing and may be given in evidence. Now, Wood, do you wish to say anything?' Wood did want to say something, and he began by recounting everything which he had already told Ruby. He took the police through all the details down to the time when he left Phyllis on the Monday. As he spoke, the Inspector took down his words.

'. . . I have never seen Phyllis since. On Wednesday I left work about 6.20 and went straight home, and afterwards walked up to Holborn with my sweetheart, Miss Ruby Young, who had called for me. We had tea at Lyons, remaining there until about eight or eight-thirty. After wandering about the West End I bade her good night, at Brompton Oratory, and returned by tube to Holborn. I then walked home from there, and arrived, as near as I can recall, about midnight.'

He went on to describe how he had first heard of the murder from Mr Moss, and how, although he had seen the photograph in the paper, he had failed to recognise it. But he said that from what he read in the papers he knew that the murder victim must be the girl he had been with. He recounted his discussions with his brother; told of the letter they had written; gave the accommodation address and concluded his statement by saying that the postcard was the only form of writing he had ever sent the girl. A new edition of the daily papers was justified. The police had detained a man, even though it was only for investigation. Somewhere in the dim recesses of Fleet

Street a reporter extolled in his latest article his previous accuracy in forecasting an 'imminent arrest'. That was only three weeks ago, when, if the truth were known, the police had never heard of Wood. But in the newspaper world 'imminence' is a relative term.

On the day following his arrest Wood was put up for identification. About fifteen men, peacefully making their way to business, were swooped upon by the police and taken into the police station to assist. When all was ready and Wood was standing among them, the ship's cook was taken to the room where they were gathered. He went to Wood and identified him as the man he had seen with Dimmock in the Rising Sun on the Monday. Clarke was the next to take his turn and he also identified Wood as the man he had seen in the Rising Sun on Monday, 9 September, talking to Emily Dimmock. The last person was the redoubtable Crabtree. For him it was an airing from gaol, but not a welcome one. He took neither pleasure nor pains in assisting the police, and went to view the men with a heavy heart. Had he been going to identify a felonious policeman from among fifteen others with a view to hanging him, he would have gone about his task most joyfully; in truth, he would have identified all sixteen as being the felons. He trudged into the room, looked along the row, spoke never a word and trudged out again.

'Well,' said Inspector Neil, 'can you recognise anyone?'

'There's a bloke in there wot knew Phyllis Dimmock, but the man I referred to in me statement's not there,' he grumbled.

'Very well,' said the Inspector, 'will you pick out the man you can identify, please?'

'No, I bloody well won't. I'm no copper's nark. I came here to pick out the bloke I mentioned in my statement – Scottie – and you 'aven't got 'im. I'm not pickin' out anyone else.'

It was a difficult situation to bring a man from a prison in which you had incarcerated him and ask him to assist in catching another criminal, even a suspected murderer.

'Look here, Crabtree. I've got something else to do,' said Neil. 'You were called here to say whether you could recognise anyone associated with Dimmock, and not to pick out Scottie. Now go inside and show me this man.'

'You coppers are all the same. Never trust a copper: even me old muvver used to tell me that.' Rumbling and grumbling, he went back into the room, walked up to Wood and said, 'This is him. He knew Dimmock, but he isn't the man I was talkin' about.'

The identification parade was finished and the men, excluding Wood, were sent to go about their business.

A few hours later Inspector Neil went back again to Wood.

'Wood,' he said, 'I have made enquiries and find that your statement as to being with Miss Ruby Young on the Wednesday night is untrue. This is a photograph of a portion of a letter. It appears to have been sent for the purpose of making an appointment for a man to meet the deceased woman on the night of her death. Your father and brother are unable to say whether you were at home that night. In consequence, I shall charge you with wilfully murdering her.'

Wood was very white, and very drawn in appearance, but his voice was steady when he replied. 'This handwriting' – he was holding the photograph – 'is certainly very like my own; in fact, I should call it a good imitation. If the young lady denies I was in her company, I cannot help it. One cannot be correct on all such small details, but I have told you the truth and I cannot do more.'

He was later taken to Kentish Town Police Station and formally charged. What he said in reply to the charge was almost inaudible, but it sounded as though he was asking if any further explanation was required.

The 'imminent arrest' had become an accomplished fact, although the 'imminence' was slightly extended. All London was agog; in fact everywhere in town and country, old and young were beginning to discuss the Camden Town murder with renewed vigour. The press made the most of it. Sensations were few and far between and this promised good copy for weeks to come. The double life: respectable by day, consorting with a prostitute by night; the search which had been outlined in the press as it progressed; the fact that his 'sweetheart' had started the trail which led to the arrest. It was an absorbing story, but there was, as ever, a side the public did not see, for back in King's Cross an old man sat heartbroken and ill: old George Wood was a broken man; the finger of public accusation was pointing at his son.

Chapter VII

The magistrates', or petty sessional, courts found in English towns had become, in 1907, so monopolised by police business that in the eyes of the public they were in name and substance the 'police courts'. It was an unfortunate title, and a misnomer, for it implied that the Court came under the domination of the police; by innuendo, it was something of a calumny on the magistrate, who daily, without fear or favour, administered justice to high and low alike. The daily routine of these courts was one of sordidness and obscurity, drunkenness and petty theft, soliciting and matrimonial disputes. But, occasionally, a *cause célèbre* found its way before the magistrate, and the Court took on an air of substantial importance.

It is one of the duties of the magistrate, at the outset of a case destined to be tried by jury, to hear the evidence for the prosecution and to decide whether a case has been made out against the accused; to determine, that is, whether there is that amount of evidence as would enable a reasonable jury of his fellow men to convict him if the prosecution's evidence stood uncontested. If there is, the magistrate commits him for trial to a higher court; if there is not, he dismisses the charge.

Mr Bross, the magistrate at Clerkenwell, had taken his seat on the morning of 7 October 1907, with a special remembrance of the importance of his position. For before him stood Robert Wood, charged with the murder of Emily Dimmock. The public portion of the Court was crowded, although it was known that the merest formality would be involved at this first hearing; the reporters were in bountiful attendance, and policemen with later cases to be heard, crowded into the little

Court to listen to the opening stages of what promised to be a particularly fascinating trial.

In the small railed dock in the centre of the Court stood Wood, his composure regained, but white and restless. At the bench in front of him sat Arthur Newton, who was to defend him. Arthur John Edward Newton was then forty-seven years of age and carried on practice as a solicitor at No. 24 Great Marlborough Street. He had previously been in partnership but had started his own practice in 1887 and was regarded as one of the leading police court solicitors of his time.

That, indeed, was how such practitioners were known in those days, not only to the public but to the legal profession, which looked askance at those who practised in the police courts. Today, the practice of the criminal law is regarded as being no more than the practice of a particular branch of the law, as indeed it is and should be. However, in the earlier 1900s and for long afterwards, the criminal lawyer – whether barrister or solicitor – was not regarded as representing the cream of the profession and the police court practitioner was quite beyond the pale.

Arthur Newton, in the end, did little during his life to improve that image. A most competent advocate, he was instructed in many of the criminal *causes célèbres* of that time. He was to represent Hawling Harvey Crippen, when he was charged, convicted and hanged for the murder of his wife, whose remains he had cut up and concealed. His lady friend Ethel Le Neve, who was charged with him, was acquitted. This case – in 1910 – brought Newton into trouble with his professional body, the Law Society.

Once a person is convicted, his solicitor is only permitted to interview him for the purpose of an appeal or to advise him in connection with his legal affairs. When Crippen was serving a reprieve from the sentence of death passed on him, Newton was afforded such an interview to advise him on the regulation of his affairs, in particular concerning his will and his decision that Ethel Le Neve (to whom he had left his estate) should replace Newton as his executor, since she had been acquitted.

Horatio Bottomley, a Member of Parliament who owned a

notorious magazine called *John Bull* – and who himself ultimately went to prison – had been conducting a campaign designed to suggest that Crippen could not have acted alone. It
was said that Crippen could not have disposed of the body
without help in the time available, and the clear implication
was that Ethel Le Neve – although acquitted – had been his
accomplice. Bottomley had in the closing stages of the trial paid
a sum of fifty guineas to Newton – ostensibly towards Crippen's defence – and Newton was found to have been a party to
the fabrication of a letter which, it was falsely purported, had
been handed to him when he interviewed Crippen in prison.
The letter, which was published in *John Bull*, contained
nothing of any significance, but the transmission to *John Bull* of
this letter was in breach of prison regulations.

As a result the Law Society's Disciplinary Committee found
Newton guilty of professional misconduct – and after he had
lost on appeal to the King's Bench Division of the High Court
he was suspended from practice for twelve months, Mr Justice
Darling commenting that if the sentence erred at all it was on
the side of leniency.

As a result of his difficulties with the Law Society and his
exceedingly extravagant lifestyle, Newton found himself short
of money and facing a financial crisis. He believed his salvation
was to be found by collaborating with some of the less than
salubrious characters whom he represented. He therefore
assisted a man called Berkeley Bennett to pass himself off as
one of the Gordon Bennetts who owned an American newspaper. Bennett induced an Austrian to part with large sums of
money for the purchase of a non-existent forest in Canada.
When the Austrian chanced to meet an actual member of the
Gordon Bennett family, the truth – as it often does – came out.
Newton found himself, accompanied by Bennett, sitting in a
part of the Old Bailey in which he was not accustomed to be,
namely the dock, and subsequently, on 24 July 1913, Newton
was sentenced to three years' penal servitude for conspiracy to
defraud the Austrian and, as a result, was struck off the Rolls of
Solicitors.

That, however, was for the future. Meanwhile, Wood's
employers had poured scorn on the suggestion that he could

be guilty of murder and, to show their faith, had put £1,000 at the disposal of Mr Newton to defray the costs of the defence.

Once an accused person is brought before a criminal court, it rests with the magistrates who will hear the committal proceedings to decide whether the accused shall meanwhile be held in custody or be released on bail.

Thus, on 7 October 1907, Newton, confident of the outcome, was applying to the presiding magistrate for bail, and was considerably taken aback by Inspector Neil's reply in opposing his application. Neil told the Court that Wood had been identified that morning as having left No. 29 St Paul's Road in the early hours of 12 September. In the face of this statement the magistrate refused to grant Newton's application.

What Neil had said was entirely true. Before leaving for the Court, the police had gathered in another ten businessmen and put Wood among them. Waiting in the station were Miss Raven (the barmaid from the Eagle), May Campbell (a lady who claimed to be able to identify both Robert Wood and the gentleman called Scotch Bob but was not later a witness at the trial), and MacCowan, who had passed St Paul's Road looking for work. They were taken into the yard where the parade was assembled, and asked to identify the persons mentioned in their statements. Unlike today, the witnesses were gathered together in the presence of those lined up for the identification parade. Wood, dressed in a blue serge suit, was wearing a bowler hat. Neither Miss Raven nor May Campbell met with any success, and MacCowan said he was unable to identify anyone by features. At the request of the Inspector, the paraded men began to walk about, whereupon MacCowan went to Wood, and indicated him as the man he had seen leaving No. 29 on 12 September. It was a severe blow, and if his evidence was upheld would inevitably lead Wood to the gallows. But it did not end there, for after MacCowan had touched Wood, May Campbell said she could now recognise him and went towards him. However, her identification was so unreliable that she was never called as a witness.

Meanwhile, the coroner's inquest – at which the Crown, in view of the public interest aroused, was represented by Sir Charles Mathews, Senior Counsel to the Treasury – proceeded from adjournment to adjournment, whilst the coroner's officer collated the evidence for the inquest. The coroner's inquiry is intended only to ascertain the identity of the deceased where, amongst other things, he or she has met violent or sudden death, so as to determine when, where and how he or she died. The coroner's officer, usually a police constable, collects evidence for the coroner and cannot get access to the fruits of other police enquiries. Thus, in the course of the inquest, Newton asked Inspector Neil, who was giving evidence, to confirm that Wood had an unblemished character; the Inspector replied, 'I have made enquiries. I would rather not answer.' On 28 October the coroner's jury returned a verdict in these terms: 'We find that the deceased Emily Elizabeth Dimmock met her death by wilful murder, and that the evidence we have received is sufficient to commit the accused to trial.'

At that time such a verdict required Wood to stand trial at the Assize Court. It was then one of the faults of the English system of criminal procedure that a coroner's jury, untrammelled by normal rules of evidence and often presided over by a coroner without legal training, was able to conduct an investigation into a crime which better qualified courts were already investigating. But the practice, which obtained for many years, of adjourning the coroner's hearing until the conclusion of the criminal proceedings did not operate in 1907. Instead, as happened in Wood's case, the magistrate adjourned his proceedings until the inquest had been concluded. (The power which a coroner possessed, concurrently with the powers of the magistrates, to commit a person for trial on a criminal charge has long since been abolished.)

By now, the police had completed their chain of evidence and not the least important link was the evidence of Lambert. He was the person who had seen Wood in the Eagle on the evening of 11 September, and his statement made Wood the last person to have been seen with the girl prior to her death. There were witnesses who declared that far from Wood having met Dimmock for the first time that Friday night, as Wood asserted, they had seen them together often and long before. Adding to the defence difficulties were the lying statements Wood had made about his movements on the Wednesday night. What had begun as a picnic was rapidly developing into a last supper.

Evidence was piling up. Ruby, who had once loved Wood, had divulged the full story under constant but proper pressure. She insisted that she did not realise her disclosures would result in the arrest of her one-time lover. But it was wrested from her and she repeated it in the police court, affirming that Wood had a peculiar walk and jerked his shoulder forward as he moved.

Newton fought desperately to avoid committal for trial but it was a hopeless task. The evidence in the magistrate's court was overwhelming. All the prosecution witnesses, however, did not fare well. MacCowan had some awkward moments. He had said that although a dark night he had seen Wood quite clearly, by the light of the electric lamp on the opposite side of the road.

'Are you positive of that?' asked the skilful Newton in a slow and rising voice.

'Yes,' MacCowan replied, 'I'm positive.'

'You will agree with me that if the light had been out, you would have been unable to see him?'

'Any fool could tell you that,' was the impolite answer.

Newton ignored the riposte.

'Then, Mr MacCowan,' he went on, producing a chart of the light timings from the Electric Light Company, 'can you explain to me how it is that the Electric Light Company say they switched the lights off at 4.37 and yet you were not there until about five minutes to five?' MacCowan was shaken, but Newton's advocacy could not alter the decision and Wood was duly committed to stand trial at the next sessions at the Old Bailey.

No. 12 Frederick Street, Gray's Inn Road, where the Woods lived, was a sad home. It was a bitter pill for old George Wood to swallow. He had made his way honestly and proudly through life and his greatest pride had been his good name. In fifty years he had known only two employers. He looked forward to leaving that unsullied name to those he loved, and it had been his greatest joy that his children showed every promise of perpetuating the good work which he had done. The sins, if only venial ones, of the son had already descended on the father. It was an inversion of the old aphorism.

He could not begin to believe that the charges levelled against his son had any basis. He wracked his brain to recall what had occurred on 11 September. It was all very well for advocates to stand in court and comment adversely on the inability of witnesses to remember anything of a particular day. It was so very easy to question, but a different matter to recollect. He talked it over with his stepson James for many hours. After careful thought they made their way to Newton's office, while the police court proceedings were still in progress.

'I've been thinking and thinking this matter overrr,' said George Wood to Newton, in his deep Scots accent. 'I think I can place the day you ask'd me about.'

'Do you mean 11 September?'

'Yes. You see, it would have been the Monday when I left my work on account of the goot. The following day the doctor came and gave me a wee bottle of linament for my foot but on the Wednesday it was upset on the carpet.'

'Well, how does that help?'

'Weel now, it's like this. My son Robert slept in the next room. Each night he would wait on me to get the alarum clock from my room. I mind him collecting the clock on the Wednesday.'

'But why are you sure it was the Wednesday? You see, you told the police you could not be sure if he was in that night or not.'

'Aw! Well, you see I had no thought about it then. I know it was Wednesday because it was then that I spilt the linament.'

'Yes,' interrupted James, 'when Dad referred to this it brought it back to my mind. I am almost sure it was the Wednesday night that Bob came in about midnight.'

'That's a matter of great importance,' said Newton.

'But, Mr Newton, that's not all. There's a Mr Rogers waiting outside who lives in the basement of our house. He came to see me. He's an angler, and he says he was away fishing on 15 September, a Sunday, and that on the Wednesday before he was in his garden about twelve o'clock at night gathering worms. He's sure that he saw my son Robert come in at that time. That would be the 11th and the night you asked about.'

Newton at once began to reduce the statements of the old man and his stepson to writing. As they finished and Newton told them he would interview Mr Rogers on his own, George Wood drew his chair closer to Newton's desk.

'Now, Mr Newton,' he said, 'I'm an old man and have taken some hard knocks in my time. I've no knowledge of these sort of happenings. Will you tell me what happens now and just what, like, are my son's chances. I want to know the truth. It's better to ken it now than be surprised later on.'

'I'll do what I can, Mr Wood, but it's no easy matter, I'm afraid. As you know the proceedings in the police court are now concluded and your son's case will be heard at the Old Bailey. I shall continue, and you must do the same, to seek out any evidence which will support Robert's statement that he was at home on that night. Now we shall have to instruct counsel. As I told Robert, and he has agreed, I am going to give this case to Marshall Hall. He's the man for this, of that there's no doubt. I regard him as the finest jury advocate at the Bar.'

'Shall we have to go and see him?' asked the father.

'I am afraid not, since barristers are not permitted to interview the witnesses they are to call, other than expert witnesses, but I shall prepare a brief. That will give counsel most of the information which he requires. It contains all the statements of the witnesses and my observations, which will include all you have just told me. From this, counsel prepares himself to conduct the case in court.'

'I follow you, Mr Newton. Now, what are the true chances in the matter?'

'The case is more difficult than I first thought. It's no use denying that. There's no doubt that your son was frequently in this woman's company. Mr Lambert saw him with her as late as the Wednesday evening, at the Eagle. But that was not to say that he was with her later on. I was banking everything on that. Then they brought this fellow MacCowan, who says that the man who left the house in the early Thursday morning was your son. He identifies him by his walk and, I am afraid, Ruby Young has confirmed that he has a peculiar gait. As you have pointed out though, many more say that he hasn't, and we'll make the most of that. There's one thing, however, which I think you do not yet know about. A woman, May Campbell, made a statement to the police. The prosecution do not intend to call her but they have supplied us with a copy of her statement. Normally they only give us the name and address of witnesses whom they have interviewed but do not intend to call. In this case they have made an exception.' He took a document from the file which lay on the desk.

'She said', he continued, 'that she was a friend of Dimmock's, and that she saw her at four o'clock on the Wednesday. She asserted that Dimmock told her then that she had received word by letter from a man friend, that she was to meet him that night, and that he was known as "Scotch Bob". This man had a grudge against her, and she was very frightened. This May Campbell says that your son is the man "Scotch Bob".'

'Why then have the prosecution not called this woman?' asked Wood.

'I do not think they consider her reliable. You see, Shaw was at home at four o'clock, so she couldn't have seen Dimmock when she said. Just what her game is I really don't know. Crabtree knows "Scotch Bob" and he emphatically says that he isn't Robert. Not the least of the difficulties, however, is that Robert told a false story to the police about his movements on the Wednesday, and tried to get Ruby Young to do the same. The prosecution are bound to say that if he lied about his movements on the Wednesday night, and lied about his previous acquaintanceship with Dimmock, it is a fair inference that he is lying about the rest of his story. In addition to this there is Lambert, who saw your son and Dimmock together; there's the postcard, and the letter which seems to be the same writing, and that means that it must be your son's.'

The old man looked more worried than ever.

'Yes, I agree it looks black, but I know my son. They can say what they like but he didna do this murder.'

'No, Mr Wood, I'm sure he didn't, but he'll be in good hands. Of that you can be assured.

'I hope so. For the prosecution will be in good hands also.'

'Well – yes – that's so. They even brought Sir Charles Mathews into the magistrate's court. He's Senior Counsel to the Treasury, so they've bought a big gun in. It's unusual for such people to take part before a case gets to the Assizes. But never fear, we have a good team as well.'

'Will there be other barristers beside Mr Hall?' asked Charles Wood.

'Oh yes. Marshall Hall is a King's Counsel, so he's not allowed to appear in court unless what are called junior counsel are briefed as well.' Newton got up and extended his hand, to bring the interview to an end.

'Don't worry, Mr Wood, we'll see this thing through for you.'

Secreted between the turmoil of Fleet Street and the bustle of the Embankment lies the serenity of the Middle Temple. In its old-world atmosphere of sweeping arches, cobbled winding roads, quaint Dickensian shops and gabled buildings work the 'learned' members of the Bar. They chose the word 'learned' for themselves; some, indeed, are. One wanders from the stress and excitement of the Strand into its quiet dignified precincts. It is as if within its boundaries things physical seem a world apart, yet in the experience of lawyers much is seen of life and its pains and joys, its successes and failures, its fear and hopes; the whole gamut of human experiences and emotions are daily run within the chambers which comprise the Temple.

On a November morning, 1907, the chambers of No. 3 Temple Gardens were anything but serene. In those chambers worked Marshall Hall KC. The excitement was occasioned by a bundle of papers which had just been handed to him from Arthur Newton. It might seem surprising that Marshall Hall, a well-known King's Counsel, should be excited at receiving a bundle of papers, but there was something outstanding about this particular bundle. The papers in the case of *Rex* versus *Wood* had arrived at a most propitious moment in his life.

In his early years a chance visit to a celebrated trial had awakened within him a love and admiration for the pursuit of advocacy. He left Rugby School, taking with him for his battle in life an outstanding ability at cricket, an inherent ability to recognise precious gems, a fascination with firearms and an attitude of disrespect for authority. Only the most indiscreet might have attempted to foretell his future course.

It was, however, to be the Bar, and in 1882 he left Cambridge with a degree, a handsome physique, unusual personality and a sweetheart, who in the same month became his wife.

One of the early and, perhaps, tiresome tasks of every young barrister is to act as 'devil' to a more senior counsel. While the older man steps into the limelight and conducts the trial before the public, the 'devil' employs hours studying the brief, noting it, analysing the evidence and suggesting for his senior the courses of action which commend themselves to his mind, which in many cases his senior studiously ignores. Marshall Hall soon found himself with a small but welcome brief in a case of immense public interest.

From there, he advanced from strength to strength. His fluent speech, outstanding presence, ready wit and evident depth of human understanding soon brought him into the front rank of the profession, where his flamboyant and over-dramatic method of presenting cases was acceptable to an extent which would not be true today.

He knew success and happiness, and when, in his marriage, he lost his wife in deeply distressing circumstances, he knew intense sorrow as well. Indeed, so profound was the shock that his whole existence underwent a complete upheaval. Perhaps this, more than anything else in his life, was to heighten the intensity which he was to direct to every task which came to his hand; this accentuated his irascibility, which set him back in his career as an advocate.

He had remarried and had 'taken silk', as becoming a King's Counsel is known, and it was reasonable to suppose that his second marriage would resettle the disturbing element which had come into his life. But it was not so and his early defiance of authority, coupled with his later experiences, led him into repeated arguments with the judges and ultimately with persons quite as powerful and sometimes less scrupulous, the owners of newspapers.

Typical of him at that time was his reply to a judge who asked how many more speeches he was to hear from Marshall Hall on a particular matter. 'I don't think your lordship heard me,' was the heated and tactless reply, 'because your lordship did not wish to hear me.' What was at once partly his greatest strength was at the same time one of his greatest weaknesses: engaged in forensic battle, he became imbued with the justice of his client's case, as he was with his belief in his own infallibility. Nothing but his own contentions could be correct, and so sincerely did he believe this, and so carried away did he become with the belief, that he occasionally made observations which he later regretted. He made just such an observation in a libel action when opposing the *Daily Mail*, owned by the powerful Alfred Harmsworth. In the heat of his argument he remarked, 'My client may have to work for her living but her reputation is entitled to the same consideration as that of any lady in the land, including Mrs Alfred Harmsworth.' This remark was taken by Harmsworth as a personal insult, and in the event caused Marshall Hall endless trouble.

So, in spite of his unusual abilities as an advocate, his endless enthusiasm, his wit, his personal charm, his amazing successes – his mere employment, if he contained his temper, seemed to presage success – his income and standing were waning. Even those who recognised his ability and were anxious to brief him were seeking other advocates, conscious of the danger that something he might say would antagonise the judge and lose the case.

Conditions at the Bar at the turn of the century were very different from those which obtain today. Over the years the whole style of presentation of a case has changed. Then, it was often a theatrical *tour de force* which claimed the attention and approval of the jury, the profession and the public; today the style is the very antithesis of oratorical fervour. Now advocacy is prosaic by comparison.

In the early 1900s there was neither radio nor television and the cinema had not developed. The public had not been exposed to the never-ending presentation of court drama and legal discussion which is now the order of the day. Virtually the sole source of information, titillation and delectation for a prurient public was the press, and a *cause célèbre* when it hit the newspapers would be reported in the minutest detail and at the greatest length. Just as the actor responds to applause, so the advocates responded to public interest and approbation.

Marshall Hall's most famous performance was his 'scales of justice' act, when he would rise to his fullest height, and, with arms outstretched at both sides, would slowly lean his head and body, from the waist, over to one side, as he told the jury how the scales of justice could so easily be put out of balance.

That Marshall Hall, judged in the context of his times, was one of the great advocates in legal history is hardly to be denied. Today, however, his methods would bring nothing but ribald laughter, and, as the recounting of his conduct of the trial of Robert Wood shows, his technique, ability and tactical approach frequently left much to be desired. Indeed, if anyone but the redoubtable Marshall Hall had pursued some of the cross-examination in which he engaged he would have been stigmatised as an inexperienced amateur. It sometimes seemed as if he failed to observe the major requirements of sound advocacy, whenever practised, of determining the objectives, adhering to them throughout the trial and eliminating extraneous material. Charisma, flair and personality, some may suspect, played a greater part in Marshall Hall's spectacular reputation than legal knowledge and a sound command of the real techniques of advocacy.

In November 1907 his fortunes were at almost their lowest ebb. He had driven his best clients to other chambers. It was not unnatural that the advent in that month of a bundle of papers, carelessly tied with pink tape, at No. 3 Temple Gardens was an occasion for excitement. The Wood trial was the sensation of the year; it was manna from Heaven – a God-sent opportunity for restoring his fortunes by a masterly defence and of regaining by a combination of ability and tact the support of the judges.

Marshall Hall hurried into the room of his 'devil', Wellesley Orr, threw the papers on the desk and told him to concentrate solely on the case for the next three weeks. 'This is the greatest case I've ever had in my life. If you have an idea, however remote or far-fetched, come in and tell me. The man's innocent.'

'The man's innocent . . .'. How could Robert Wood be anything but innocent, now that Marshall Hall was defending him? It may have been vanity or conceit, but it was also a manifestation of one of the best assets an advocate can possess if he learns to harness it, namely an ability to condition the mind to unswerving belief in the truth of the client's story.

Wellesley Orr set to work on the papers. Obviously the most damaging evidence (apart from the lying statements which the accused himself had made) were the witnesses Lambert, Roberts and MacCowan. Lambert, seemingly honest, saw Wood with the girl on the Wednesday evening. Roberts had seen them together and remembered the card and letter which Emily Dimmock had shown him as having been in the same handwriting. MacCowan purported to have seen Wood leaving No. 29 St Paul's Road in the early hours of the Thursday morning. He turned the problem which confronted him around in his mind, endeavouring to view it from every angle. In due course he went to Marshall Hall's room.

'Marshall, I think I'm on to something.'

'Good! What is it? Sit down and tell me.'

'However foolish, so we contend, the reason Wood lied about his movements was to cover his liaison with this woman; if Wood is exonerated, the next under grave suspicion is Roberts, for he was with her during the three previous nights. What's more he was waiting for her in the Rising Sun on the Wednesday night.'

'Yes. So?'

'Well, consider May Campbell. She volunteers a description during the early stages of the investigation and tells a story, patently untrue, of her meeting in the afternoon with Dimmock. She says that Wood is Scotch Bob and that Dimmock said he had sent her a letter telling her to meet him and that she was frightened.'

Marshall sat listening, but heard nothing new.

'How did May Campbell know that Dimmock had received that letter?' asked Orr.

'I expect she met Dimmock and Dimmock told her.'

'But we know that Dimmock was in all day, from Bert Shaw and the landlady; we know she met Wood in the evening and stayed with him until at least eleven o'clock, on his own admission. No. The point is this.' Wellesley Orr paused. 'One person who did know about the letter was Roberts. He said Dimmock showed him the letter. I do not say Roberts did the murder, but at least he knew he would come under grave suspicion, that he was the next in the line, and he may have done, at the least, what we believe Wood did, namely provide himself with an alibi in case of difficulties. Just, as we say, Wood got Ruby Young to give a false statement, so Roberts went to May Campbell, unfolded the story which she ultimately related and told her about the letter he'd seen. Although she could not give a description when first interviewed by the police, she later gave a description of the man, but couldn't pick Wood out until MacCowan had done so. Marshall! It stands out a mile. I'll wager anything that May Campbell and Roberts knew one another well, and she had tried to pass on to Roberts a description of the man with whom she had gathered that Emily Dimmock was sometimes seen.'

Marshall Hall sat, his chin in his hand, weighing his junior's theory.

'No,' he said at last, 'it's too far-fetched. It's just possible that May Campbell had met Dimmock. In any case Roberts is a most dangerous witness; far best to leave him alone.'

Wellesley Orr did not argue further; he knew it would achieve no more and left the room. But he also knew that, although Marshall had dismissed his theory, that did not mean it would not be reconsidered. He knew Marshall. It would stay in his mind, and before long he might come to his way of seeing it. It was in keeping with Marshall Hall's temperament and character that he was easily swayed from an opinion. A momentary thought would find him throwing a carefully planned line of cross-examination to the four winds and embarking on some new and adventurous course.

At the very next conference which Marshall Hall had with Newton, he told him, as if he had just thought of it, that he could now see it all quite clearly. Why! Roberts, the ship's

cook, and May Campbell had got together; Roberts had persuaded her to try and protect him. It was the same as with
Wood and Ruby; it was as clear as day. Newton was no easier
to convince than Marshall Hall when Orr first broached the
matter to him. He argued strenuously with the KC and, by the
time he left, Hall had reverted to his former opinion.

While Newton was busy endeavouring to unearth fresh facts
to assist the defence, and Orr was carefully scrutinising the
evidence, a heavier problem was facing Marshall Hall. Until
1898, it was not possible, except in a few special crimes, for an
accused person to give evidence on oath and thus subject
himself to cross-examination. Long and heated disputes pre-
ceded the passing of the Criminal Evidence Act, which in that
year made such a course possible. It was asserted, on the one
hand, that it would carve a deep inroad into the whole struc-
ture of British justice, founded as it was on principles of fair
play for the accused; on the other hand it was contended that
an innocent person had nothing to fear from cross-examination. By 1907, no person who had elected to go into the
witness box and give evidence in his own defence had been
acquitted, perhaps for the good reason that no person charged
with a capital offence had expressed a desire to take the oath.

It may perhaps be added that subsequent experience has
fully justified the enactment, for while judges have found that
it has increased perjury by prisoner witnesses to an appreci-
able extent, it has now long been recognised that although the
opportunity to give evidence has often been the terror of the
guilty, it has obviously provided a shield for the innocent.
However, in November 1907, Marshall Hall faced the task of
deciding whether to call Robert Wood. If he failed to do so it
might invite undesirable comment from the judge that Wood
had failed to substantiate his story on oath. The right to make
such a comment was forbidden to the prosecutor, but if Wood
went into the witness box he would have to face cross-examination by Sir Charles Mathews, an experienced prosecutor.
Added to that was the knowledge that he was a self-confessed
liar who had sought to manufacture a false alibi.

Shortly before the trial, as is the custom, a consultation was
arranged between the 'leader', the juniors and the solicitor.

One by one the junior counsel arrived at Marshall Hall's chambers: first Herman Cohen, then Huntly Jenkins with J.F. Lort Williams; Wellesley Orr had not been briefed, but because he had taken such great part and interest in the matter, special permission was obtained from Newton, despite the fact that he had not been formally instructed, to enable him to assist with the case and to attend. Marshall Hall sat at his desk, the junior counsel around him, and slightly apart Arthur Newton and his clerk. Every aspect of the matter was discussed, the weaknesses considered, the stratagems formulated. Finally they arrived at the teasing question, 'Should Wood be called into the witness box?' Marshall Hall thought not; the lesser beings found themselves involuntarily agreeing. But not Orr – he persisted in his belief that Wood must be called. At last he got to his feet, and said with some solemnity, 'Marshall, unless you call him, Wood will hang as high as Haman.'

The KC stared at him as if trying to divine the inner reasons for the great conviction with which Orr spoke. Then, slowly nodding his head, saying, 'No, I think not,' he rose from his chair. The consultation was at an end, but anyone knowing Marshall Hall would have been rash to regard the course of the defence as settled.

On 10 December 1907 the case had been brought before the Grand Jury, as was then the practice. Despite the need for magistrates to satisfy themselves that sufficient evidence existed to justify sending an accused for trial by jury, to say nothing of the power of coroners to send cases of unlawful homicide for trial, a Grand Jury intervened as well. This consisted of twenty-three men of substantial position. They were subjected to an address called 'a charge' by one of the High Court judges, when a bill of indictment (a formal written accusation of a criminal offence against someone) was placed before them. The Grand Jury considered the allegations in secret, hearing only as much of the prosecution's evidence as they desired, and in Wood's case duly found 'a true bill' against him on the charge of murder. This means that they considered it appropriate for him to be tried by judge and jury. Grand Juries were abolished in 1933 without any mourning for their passing.

Chapter VIII

On 12 December 1907, the eyes of the public were centred on the new Central Criminal Court, Old Bailey. During the morning a crowd had been congregating outside the building. At the public entrances, through which access was to be had to the court galleries, stood a line of would-be spectators. The passer-by, with other business, might gaze at the shining and blindfolded statue of Justice above the magnificent dome. The more fortunate citizen, to whom a special invitation had been granted, passed between the police standing at the main door, mounted the steps, made his way through the swing door and found himself in the hall. Around him was a symphony of wood panelling and marble. As he climbed the staircase to the upper hall, he was impressed – as he was intended to be – by the full majesty of the law. There was nothing on the upper floor to detract from his first impressions: the dome with its colourful paintings; the panelled interior of the entrances; the marble floor; the hubbub of the witnesses and officials; the swish of the robes as the white-wigged barristers – and a few not so white – crossed from the robing rooms to the courts; the police – the constables appearing very nervous, the detectives very important; the women sitting on the benches – the relations of prisoners, worried, anxious, and some crying or with tear-stained eyes – the sensation-seekers, agog with expectations.

Of the four courts (there are now nineteen), it was noticeable that one was attracting more people towards it and had more attendants and police guarding the door. It was the Court in which Robert Wood was to face a jury of twelve just men and true, and answer, if they so ordained, with the most precious of possessions: his life. It was not yet ten o'clock but the Court was filled with a mass of chattering people. In the centre stood the spacious dock with its high wooded sides surmounted by glass. On either side were the benches for witnesses and jurors in waiting, occupied by the friends of lawyers whose special connection with the courts had enabled them to secure access. Between the dock and the Bench were the places for the actors in the drama. On one side, counsel for the prosecution; as yet his place was vacant, but on his desk rested a large bundle of papers majestically tied with white tape, as is the custom with Treasury briefs.

Counsel for the prosecution, who most unusually had also attended the inquest and the magistrate's court, was Sir Charles Mathews, born in New York, the son of a three-times-married actress. Mathews had assumed the name of his stepfather, and on leaving Eton had entered Montague Williams's chambers, as a pupil, Williams later declaring that he was the best pupil he had ever had. He had unsuccessfully sought to enter Parliament as a Liberal, but he was later, from 1908 until his death, Director of Public Prosecutions. A small man, with a weak and unpleasing voice, he was nonetheless fluent and histrionic. Dapper and precise, he shared with the Judge at the trial, and with Crabtree, a great interest in horses. He was now the Senior Treasury Counsel, that is, one of the barristers specially retained at the Old Bailey to represent the Crown in criminal trials.

Behind the bench for counsel, in the four rows of padded seats emblazoned with the arms of the City of London, sat the distinguished visitors whose admission had been by ticket. They were a formidable array: H.B.Irving, the great actor; A.E.W.Mason, the noted novelist, to hear of more unusual happenings than ever occurred at the Villa Rose; Sir George Alexander; Sir Arthur Pinero; Oscar Asche; Seymour Hicks, later to be knighted and study criminology as a hobby, and many other notabilities. In the well of the Court was the solicitors' table and nearby the table at which the police sat. At the far end of the row of tip-up seats on which the prosecutors sat were the seats for the defending counsel so that all should be facing the jury, whose box was immediately opposite them. At the back of the Court, raised and screened by the front portions of a series of medium-sized desks, would be found the Judge – above his head the sword of justice and coat of arms, on either side the aldermen and sheriffs of the City of London in their splendid robes. To complete the picture, the chair of the Clerk of the Assize stood beneath the Judge's desk; to his right were the reporters' desks. The stage was set and the actors due to make their entrances.

Every eye turned towards the figure of Marshall Hall as he swung through the doors, no one more conscious of his commanding figure than himself, followed by Sir Charles Mathews. Gradually the seats filled, the Clerk called the names of the jury summoned to the Court, then – to the accompaniment of loud knocking at the Court doors, the thunderous cry of 'Silence' from the usher and the undercurrent of noise as the Court rose to its feet – Mr Justice Grantham, the Judge, accompanied by the aldermen and sheriffs, entered the Court. The proclamation being read by the usher, the Judge took his seat, placed on the desk his bouquet of flowers, associated originally with the foul smells which in former days his predecessors had to combat, and awaited the empanelling of the jury.

By no stretch of the imagination was Robert Wood fortunate in the choice of judge to preside over his trial. The man who would contribute significantly to his ultimate fate was Sir William Grantham. Seventy-two years of age when the trial began, he had been educated at King's College School, London, and after being called to the Bar had established a busy practice on the south-eastern circuit, mostly around Sussex, without managing to make any mark in London.

The *Dictionary of National Biography*, damning him with faint praise, observed that as a junior he was very useful 'in an action on a builder's account, in a compensation case and especially in disputes in which a combined knowledge of law and horseflesh was desirable'. Indeed, he was one of the founders of the Pegasus Club, the meeting place of enthusiastic barrister horsemen, and was a notable critic of horseflesh – an attribute which would, at least, have appealed to Crabtree, whose interest in horses had taken him, on one occasion, to gaol.

Grantham had on three occasions been returned to Parliament as a Conservative: in 1874 for East Surrey, again for the same constituency in 1880 and for Croydon in 1885. A militant Tory and a typical English country gentleman and squire, he would appear at Inns of Court dinners in a scarlet coat, handed down to him from an ancestor, which was the dress of the old Bloomsbury Association or 'Devil's Own'. Before he could retake his seat in Parliament, following the election of 1885, he was made a High Court judge, more, one suspects (as often happened in those days), for political services than for legal acumen, although he had been deputy chairman, and later chairman, of East Sussex Quarter Sessions.

On the High Court Bench he frequently found himself in trouble. Well able to cope with the run-of-the-mill cases, 'he lacked the breadth of mind and the grasp of intellect for trying great and complicated issues and was a very unsatisfactory Judge in commercial cases'. He tried election petitions and was accused of showing unwarranted bias in them towards the Tories, so much that it gave rise to parliamentary debates of censure, prompting Sir Henry Campbell-Bannerman, the Prime Minister, to urge the House not to 'take the first step which must lead to nothing less than the removal of the Judge from the Bench'.

A combination of Marshall Hall's volatile temperament and aptitude for crossing judges and the autocratic militant Tory squire on the Bench offered omens for an explosive trial.

Up the stairs leading from the cells to the interior of the dock came the prisoner – Robert Wood. He walked hesitantly to the front of the dock and sat on the chair indicated by the warders. The Court, each and every member, looked at him; in return he looked firmly at the Judge. It was difficult to determine from his appearance whether he was nervous or assured; only his pale, wan face conveyed the anxiety through which he was passing, as his thoughts were interrupted by the warder whispering to him to stand. The Clerk read from the indictment: 'Robert William Thomas George Cavers Wood, you are indicted for, and stand charged on the coroner's inquisition with, the wilful murder of Emily Elizabeth Dimmock. Are you guilty or not guilty?'

'I am not guilty,' he replied. After two potential jurors had been rejected as a result of challenges by Marshall Hall, the jury was empanelled and sworn. Sir Charles Mathews rose ponderously from his seat; the fight had begun and a man's life was the stake.

Sir Charles began to outline the case in a temperate and measured manner. 'Members of the jury, we start with a fact in regard to which I think there will be no dispute, and that fact is that someone on the early morning of 12 September killed that woman.' He described the life which Phyllis had led and how she had been found. He described Wood's background, his home life and his associations of the night; he detailed the evidence which would show, he suggested, that Wood had known Dimmock since the spring of 1906; he introduced Ruby Young and her relationship to the accused, and his request to her to supply false information. Piece by piece, he brought out the facts. The meeting in the Rising Sun, the postcard, the evidence of Roberts, Lambert and MacCowan. He went on to describe the condition of the room when the body was found. 'In that room, on the table, were the remains of a supper, and it was evident that two persons had partaken of it. . . . On the wash-stand was a basin containing bloodstained water. . . . A shutter had been pulled aside to admit a narrow strip of light, the glimmer of which was directed on to a picture postcard album. The album lay open on a chair and a number of postcards were strewn about all over the floor.' He paused and leaned towards the jury, 'Gentlemen of the jury, the "Rising Sun" postcard plays an important part in this case, and perhaps no fact is so important as the fact that, whoever committed the crime, with all the dangers attendant upon staying behind where that crime had been committed, went through the postcard album for the purpose of regaining something.' Another pause. 'Why?'

He passed on to the details of the missing articles and to point out in fairness to the accused that none of them had been traced to Wood. 'But', he added, 'they would all go in a very small receptacle. It would be quite easy to dispose of the things that were stolen.' All the material evidence was explained, Wood's conduct after the discovery of the murder was described and, with a last expression of hope to the jury that they might retain an open mind until the termination of the proceedings, he concluded his address. As he called his first witness, a formal witness to identify the deceased, there were muffled whispers in Court; the tension which his skilful opening had created was momentarily relaxed.

The next witness was a plain-clothes detective who produced a plan he had drawn of St Paul's Road, showing in particular the position of the street lamps and six arc lights on the railway goods siding behind the street. His evidence was short and sufficiently uninteresting to the public to allow their attention to be diverted to the notabilities in Court. It seemed certain that Marshall Hall would waste no time with this witness. Yet he came to his feet as the prosecutor sat down, felt behind his back for the seat, tipped it back and established that on the morning of 13 September the lamps were extinguished at 4.37 a.m.

If the lights were extinguished at 4.37 a.m. 'they would be useless for lighting purposes at five minutes to five?' he asked. 'Yes,' replied the officer. Later he repeated the same question and was fortunate in getting the same affirmative answer, which he hoped might show that MacCowan, who had said at the magistrate's court that he saw a man with a strange gait leave Dimmock's home at 4.55 a.m., would appear to have had an inadequate opportunity for identification.

This accomplished, he turned on the policeman: 'Do you think that's a fair plan?'

'I do.'

Marshall Hall glanced at the witness and then at the jury. 'I put it to you, have you ever seen a more misleading plan in your life?' The witness saw no reason to reply. 'Would not anyone looking at this plan come to the conclusion that the light was reflected upon the front of 29 St Paul's Road?'

'Not on the front but in the neighbourhood.'

Marshall Hall held the plan in the air and pointed to it with his finger. 'Here is a line, but nothing to show that on the opposite side of the road there is a continuous row of houses.'

'They are not continuous. There are spaces between – they are in pairs.'

The Judge lifted his plan, put it down again.

'From the optical point of view,' the Judge asked, 'would the line be continuous or not?'

'It would be continuous.'

Marshall Hall had made his point, but it was not to be left there. 'Do you know anything about the properties of light?' The plain-clothes policeman decided he did, but only when the cross-examiner had explained that he only meant you could see things better when it was light than when it was dark.

The series of questions which followed were from time to time accompanied by a significant glance towards the jury box. When he sat down he had removed the impression that the full glare of the lights was thrown on to No. 29. Rather did it seem the reverse.

As the detective left the witness box, Bert Shaw walked towards it. It was an unenviable task for Bert. His blithe air was gone. He was greatly subdued. He little relished the task of again unbaring his secrets to the world. But he gave his evidence in a straightforward manner, describing his life with Phyllis and his discovery of her body. Whether she was his wife or not, the sympathy of the onlookers was with him; his had been a dreadful experience and Marshall Hall did not unduly worry him. It was especially unpleasant when he had to confess to knowing that Phyllis had lived in a disorderly house, but the KC quickly passed on to the search for the postcard and to question whether he ever wrote to Phyllis.

It was at this early stage in the trial that there emerged the sort of conduct of a case which must cause even the most ardent admirers of Marshall Hall's exploits some perplexity in the light of his reputation for exceptional advocacy. He was, after all, then forty-eight years of age, with twenty-three years' experience at the Bar – no mere tyro. Whatever doubts existed, certain matters were beyond controversy. First, that on the night that Emily Dimmock was murdered Bertram Shaw, her common-law husband, was in Sheffield. Secondly, that he did not write the letter, burnt fragments of which had been found in the grate of their apartment, and thirdly that the writing on the letter was identical to that on the card, which Wood had throughout readily admitted was his.

No possible purpose could be served by the defence challenging those incontrovertible facts. The youngest and most inexperienced advocate would never so much as consider doing so. Yet Marshall Hall – in a stern and almost bullying manner – put to Shaw in cross-examination: 'There were two or three of you searching for a postcard [on the morning of the discovery of the body] which you knew existed and you never lifted the paper which it was natural it might have got underneath?'

'No.'

'You were looking for a postcard, and do you mean to say you never pulled the paper out?'

'I do not remember.'

'Did you know that Roberts had said the postcard shown to him by Dimmock was signed "Bert"?' (He had already elicited from the witness that he usually signed letters 'Bert', but Roberts had never said that the postcard was signed 'Bert', though he had said the letter which had been burned was so signed.)

'I was told so.'

'And that was the name she always called you?'

'Yes.'

'As a matter of fact, did you write to her?'

'No.'

'Do you swear it?'

'Yes.'

'Did you not write from Sheffield that night?'

'No.'

'Have you ever written to her?'

'Yes.'

'And always signed yourself "Bert"?'

'Yes.'

When Mathews re-examined, he asked Shaw, 'Was the fragment of the letter found in the grate in your handwriting?'

'No.'

'Do you know whose it is?'

'No. I had never seen it before.'

The only sensible and reasonable explanation of this line of cross-examination was to suggest to the jury that Shaw had written the letter, the charred remains of which had been found, and that he had deliberately avoided finding the postcard to avoid comparison, presumably to imply that he had written that as well. What other possible purpose could such questions serve?

Yet Marshall Hall interrupted Mathews's re-examination to say it might save time if he admitted there was no question that the handwriting on the fragment produced was that of the accused. 'I never suggested', he asserted, 'that the witness Shaw wrote the letter.'

This was too much for the Judge. 'I am glad that you have made that statement, Mr Marshall Hall,' he said, 'because I understood from the cross-examination that you suggested the witness had written this letter.' Marshall Hall continued to deny this. The Judge was undeterred. 'I am glad you make that statement,' he repeated, 'because you asked the witness if he wrote her from Sheffield that night.'

'I do not intend', said Marshall Hall, 'to suggest that he wrote the letter.'

The altercation ended with Marshall Hall accepting that Shaw was in Sheffield that night. He added, 'My object in asking the questions I did will be seen later.' It never was. The whole line of questioning seems irrational, since it could hardly be calculated to impress the jury with the reliability of the defence or its advocate.

Shaw left the box, his appearance indicating that he hoped never to return; yet by comparison with those who were to meet the KC at a later date, his ordeal was a light one.

Mrs Stocks, who was followed by her husband, gave evidence of Phyllis's movements on the day of the murder, and of her previous life in the house. It is an age-old trick of advocacy to endeavour to take the sting from the cross-examiner's whip. Questions which may seem of great importance when elicited by the defence, may appear relatively unimportant when gratuitously tendered by the prosecution. No doubt anticipating that Marshall Hall might suggest that she was an unreliable witness, who must have known something of Phyllis's behaviour, Sir Charles Mathews asked, 'Were you satisfied that Shaw and Dimmock were respectable when they first came?'

Mrs Stocks placed her arms across her chest, opened and shut her mouth with a staccato crack, 'I was.'

'Why were you satisfied?'

The mouth cracked open and shut again, 'Because I saw their rent book when they first came.' The passport to society; the jury understood. But Sir Charles was mistaken; both the landlady and her husband left the box with their evidence virtually uncontested.

Another surprise was to follow. Marshall Hall was noted for his special knowledge of medical matters and for his ability in dealing with medical witnesses. His father had been a doctor and he had acquired considerable knowledge from him. It was to be expected that he would question Dr Thompson, the Divisional Surgeon, at length, but he asked even fewer questions of him. In the main they sought to establish that the razors found in the room were unlikely to have been used since no blood was found on them. The doctor's evidence was inconclusive on this point. He repeated his original views, formed when he first saw the body, adding that, judging by the condition of the stomach, Phyllis had been murdered about three hours after partaking of food, and that while uncertain of the time of death, which must have been instantaneous, it was his opinion that she must have been dead for several hours – seven or eight perhaps. He saw the body at 1 p.m., which put the time of death at around 5 to 6 a.m. This was an estimate of time which Marshall Hall had no desire to see changed.

The luncheon adjournment over, the Court was about to resume. Roberts walked in, nervous, alert, darting furtive glances as he made his way to the witness box.

'What's your name?' asked the Clerk.

'Robert Percival Roberts,' he replied.

'Take the Bible in your right hand,' continued the Clerk in a mournful tone. 'Do you swear by Almighty God that the evidence which you will give shall be the truth, the whole truth and nothing but the truth?'

The solemn tone was transmitted to Roberts, the ship's cook.

'I do, so help me Gawd.' Roberts would need all the help which he could muster, for he was the witness who might substantiate or disprove Orr's theory, assuming Marshall Hall had accepted it; all indications were that he had dismissed it from his mind. But as the witness was being sworn, he leaned towards Wellesley Orr, who had volunteered his assistance at the trial, and whispered, 'I thought you'd like to know I'm going to call Wood and I'm going to cross-examine this witness on your lines.'

Sir Charles slowly took Roberts through his evidence, from his meeting with Dimmock to his visits to St Paul's Road on the Sunday and Monday. Roberts described how she had shown him the 'Rising Sun' postcard, and by the time he came to Tuesday's events every person in Court was leaning forward in his seat.

'When did you next meet Dimmock?'

'On the Tuesday evening. We went to the theatre, then to the Rising Sun, and back to St Paul's Road.'

'Did she show you any more cards or letters?'

'No. But the following morning, I heard a knock at the door and two letters were shoved underneath.'

'Where were you?'

'I was still in bed.'

'Yes? Well, what happened then?'

'She opened the letters, one was an advert from a tailor or sumfink, the other she showed me.'

'Why?'

'Well, she went to the top drawer, took out the postcard and showed me that, with the letter. They were the same 'and-writing.'

'Do you remember sufficient of the letter to repeat some of its contents?'

'Yes! It covered the first three sides of the sheet.' The sheet, he implied, was folded in two so as to provide four sides. He paused and looked to the ceiling as if in deep thought, scratched his head, and then continued, 'Yes, let me see, on the third page I remember seeing "Dear Phyllis, Will you meet me at the bar of the Eagle at Camden Town 8.30 tonight Wednesday – Bert".'

The Judge looked perplexed, nor was he alone in his perplexity. 'Was that all there was on the letter?' he asked.

'No. That was on the third page, your lordship. I never saw the uvver pages.'

The Judge's mind was still unclear. 'Then you only saw part, but that was a complete letter in itself, beginning "Dear Phyllis" and ending "Bert".'

'Yes.'

In response to Sir Charles the witness offered his description of Phyllis burning the letters, moving on to the time when he left the house, to the identification parade, and to his statement to the police. The turn of the defence had arrived. Roberts did not relish it. He preferred the bar of the Eagle with a pint of mild in his fist to standing in a Court of Justice facing a different sort of bar. There to the front of him was the towering frame of Marshall Hall; his glaring eyes seeming to sear into Roberts's brain; he felt like a rabbit faced by a giant ferret. His fear was apparent even before the cross-examination began.

'Tell me, Roberts,' began Marshall Hall, 'do you know a woman named May Campbell?'

'By sight – yes.' Roberts did not expect these questions.

'Have you ever spoken to her?'

'Yes.'

'Did she give you a description of a man who she said was known as a friend of Dimmock?'

Roberts's voice dropped perceptibly. 'Yes.' Orr had been correct: the nexus between them was established.

'Did that description correspond very much with your description of the accused?'

'Yes, it did.'

'So you could have picked him out from May Campbell's description of him?'

'Not unless I knew him.'

'Did she add in her description "Pimples on the face and neck"?'

'She said something about pimples. Pimples don't always stay there.'

'Don't argue,' thundered Marshall. 'Were you not in a great fright when you heard of the murder?'

'No, I was not.'

'Did you not realise that next to the murder—'

Roberts did not allow Marshall Hall to finish. '—I was next to 'im?'

'Yes?'

'Yes, I did. That's why I stayed in the Rising Sun. I said I'd stay there till the police arrived.'

The second point of Orr's theory was established. First, Roberts knew May Campbell; secondly, he was frightened because he was next on the list. They passed to other matters.

'Why should the girl want you to compare the letter with the postcard?'

''Ow do I know!'

'You have sworn that the part of the letter you repeated was written on the third sheet and that the fourth sheet was blank.' Roberts had turned his eyes to the floor and was examining his boots. Again the thunderous voice of the KC rumbled across the Court. 'Look up, man! We're in a Court of Justice. Don't hang your head. Now – have you not sworn that?'

'Yes, but—'

'Look at this piece of paper. It appears to be torn from a notebook or scribbling book, doesn't it?'

'Yes. You must think I've got a tremendous intellect to remember all these things. I was told to describe the letter and I did it to the best of me ability.'

'Will you swear that it was a letter and not a piece of paper torn from a memorandum book?'

'I will.'

'I put it to you the story of this long letter is an invention?'

'It's not so.'

'Are you quite certain about the contents?'

'Yes.'

'Repeat it again.'

'"Dear Phyllis, Will you meet me at the bar of the Eagle at Camden Town 8.30 tonight, Wednesday – Bert".'

'How could anybody writing that on the Tuesday write "tonight" for Wednesday?'

'You generally write that way to let a person know.'

'What! When writing on a Tuesday to make an appointment for a Wednesday write "meet me tonight"?'

'I don't—' stammered Roberts.

The witness was in a fix; from the back of the Court came a ripple of laughter. Marshall Hall swung round to the direction from which it came. 'Don't laugh,' he cried, 'I implore you not to laugh – a man's life is at stake.' A sudden respectful silence greeted his outburst. Marshall turned back to the witness and suggested that he had said it was signed 'Bert' in order to throw suspicion on Shaw. Roberts denied it, but he admitted that although he said the letter which Phyllis had shown him had a blank page, the burned piece which the barrister showed to him had some writing upside down, as if the writer was cramped for space.

'Did you not see Dimmock at all on the Wednesday night?'

'No.'

'Are you prepared to say that you were not in her company at all that night?'

'Yes. I can give the name of a man who knows what time I went home that night.' Marshall Hall turned to Orr, and after a whispered conversation sat down. The re-examination of the witness by Sir Charles Mathews was short. Before he called his next witness he looked enquiringly at Mr Justice Grantham. The Judge looked at the clock.

'Yes, Sir Charles, I think that will do for today. Ten-thirty tomorrow.' Counsel bowed, the usher shouted 'Silence', the Court came to its feet again, and with his robes flowing around him the Judge left.

The jurors, witnesses and public wandered out of the courtroom. They stood chatting in the halls, watching the celebrities leave the building. They made their routes through the vast doors and passages, while the prisoner descended the narrow stairs leading to the cells. It was a commentary on their positions. The public, flowing carelessly from the building to which they had been voluntarily attracted by a combination of curiosity and a desire for entertainment, made their way into the London streets, through the gathering darkness, the light mist and the cold, sharp wintry air to the warmth and comfort of their fires and homes; by train, carriage, car and foot they departed to the freedom of their family.

The prisoner made his way to his cell, in handcuffs, to await conveyance to cold, unfriendly Brixton prison.

Robert Wood reached the bottom of the narrow steps, passed along the corridor, lined on each side by the heavy iron railings of the cells, to the one allotted him for the duration of his trial. The warder opened the heavy door, showed Wood inside, and clanged it back again. Wood looked through the little hatch to see if anyone was coming to see him, but after some minutes had elapsed he retired to the hard wooden seat to complete the sketches which he had made during the hearing in court. There was nothing encouraging about his surroundings: the small misshapen eating utensils, the messages on the wall – 'Though walls may not a prison make, these will do to get on with' scribbled there by some desolate accused; others were expressed in less refined terms. The dinginess of the atmosphere was depressing and upsetting.

The warder brought him a mug of thick brown tea and a hunk of bread, with a smear of butter on it. When he had taken as much as he was able, they escorted him to the vast yard, bounded on all sides by high walls, and put him into a police van. The massive wooden doors drew open. For a fleeting moment he got a glimpse of the crowds outside the gates watching his departure, and he was on his way to the loneliness of Brixton prison.

Prisons are inseparably associated with huge, high walls, and Brixton was no exception. The wall which runs along the side of the road leading to the entrance is the first part of the building which strikes the eyes. When the smaller door within the heavy main gates has been opened to allow the prisoner to enter, and then is securely shut behind him, it seems as if with that act all hope of ever passing through again must be abandoned. Air, life and hope, it seems, are forever shut out.

Under the dark, dispiriting arch, into the open yard and across to the cells. Even the prisoner on remand feels he might already have been convicted. The privileges which he receives over those of the convicted man lose value amid the ineffable gloom of his surroundings.

For Wood his ability to sketch had been a form of relaxation. The drawings which he produced were the work of a disillusioned man. In one, a woman is praying by her bed. She kneels with her face in her left hand, and in her right hand she holds a letter. Cupid is sleeping at her feet and a figure of a man hangs from the gallows in the corner. In another a game of poker is in progress between Arthur Newton and a policeman. The stakes, which are in the centre of the table, are represented by Wood in chains, a small and insignificant figure. While the game is proceeding, Cupid is whispering in the officer's ear, presumably telling him the strength of his opponent's hand and how to defeat him. His drawings exhibited no nervousness. His lines were sharp and well defined. And as the hours rolled leisurely by and his ultimate fate grew nearer determination, he sketched his moments away. Was it unconcern? Who could answer?

Familiarity with misfortune, as with other experiences, breeds contempt. When the warder had refused Wood an open razor for shaving, he gave him a safety razor. That was as much as was necessary, but some inherent, unconscious, sadistic tendency encouraged him to tell the prisoner that it was the same razor as Rayner, the young and notorious murderer, had used.

But no chances were taken in His Majesty's prisons. All sharp articles, string and bootlaces, in fact anything with which a prisoner could hang or kill himself in a moment of despair, are taken away. Occasionally he is allowed visitors, but a warder will be present to overhear. It is a special pleasure when the lawyer of an accused person visits him, for then he is allowed to remain in a visiting room without the tiresome presence of the guard.

As evening passed into night Wood sat down to write to his brother:

Dear Charles

I am just back. So sorry I could not grasp you by the hand today. Of course, I have nothing now in my possession but the clothes which I stand up in.

My feelings are strange today: such that I cannot describe, though quite peaceful. Whispers of good cheer came from every direction; and even the orderly that tends my room moved silently and with some reverence this morning.

Little did I think that one day I should appear on the capital charge, under that beautiful figure of Justice (by Frampton, R.A.) that towers above the Old Bailey. I think you have admired it. I have a memory of sitting at the same supper with this great sculptor on more than one occasion.

I liked Marshall Hall's manner when he spoke to me today, and he is apparently a splendid man. I am rather cut off now from Mr Newton, so please call his attention to any point, though I expect they view things differently from us – the legal mind, I mean.

Pardon, dear Charles, if I have omitted any due thanks or remarks. To be tried for one's life is, I find, sufficient for the day, and I am very weary. I must ask you to be of good cheer, and to take care of yourselves.

I understand that there are great odds to face that may end disastrously, but I will carry my head high. For I have done no grievous wrong.

Good-bye – fondest wishes to you all – good-bye.

Bob.

Wearily, with whispers of good cheer still reverberating in his ears, he lay down to rest on the hard prison mattress, until the next day would bring the second stage of the battle.

Chapter IX

Public interest had increased, if that were possible, when the second day of the trial opened. The jury filed back into their seats; the *Evening News* of the previous night had described them as 'the least distinguished part of the picture. An unpretentious jury of very ordinary-looking citizens who appeared to be wondering how the shop was getting on while they were away'. Mr Justice Grantham lost no time when he arrived in castigating the paper for its comments and in assuring the reading public that the jury is 'the glory of the country'. In criminal trials it certainly was and may still be, but his strictures were a little unfair, though their purpose was to show the great care which the law took to protect its juries. Old Bailey juries are not selected for their looks, and, however intriguing the case, only those called to serve on juries for weeks on end can appreciate how often thoughts fly to whether Perkins has made the books balance today.

But there they were, watching the bewigged and sometimes shabbily gowned lawyers, the solemn-faced judge, the silent, sketching prisoner, and the lodger of St Paul's Road, Mrs Lancaster, describing how, at a late day in the investigation, because she had not been asked when first seen by police, she had remembered putting two letters under Phyllis's door. She came and went, and another unimportant witness as well, and then Clarke was launched into his meetings in the Rising Sun with Roberts, the ship's cook.

Bodkin, the junior prosecution counsel, was examining him.

'Have you seen the accused before?'

'Yes, I saw him in the bar of the Rising Sun on the Monday night between a quarter to eleven and eleven o'clock.'

'What was he doing?'

'He spoke to Dimmock for about a minute, and she then returned to speak to Roberts.'

'How long was the accused there?'

'Three or four minutes. After that he went away.'

'When were you next at the Rising Sun?'

'The following night and the night after.'

'That's the Wednesday. What happened then?'

'Roberts and I stayed there until closing time. I did not see the accused or Dimmock.'

'Where did you go then?'

'Roberts and I walked home together, the landlady let us in. We spoke for about ten minutes and went to bed.'

Marshall Hall came to his feet: 'How long had you known Roberts?'

'Since Sunday, 8 September, previous to the tragedy.'

'Did Roberts not tell you he was very anxious to prove where he was on the night of the tragedy?'

'No.'

'Did you hear that he slept with Dimmock on the Monday, Tuesday and Sunday nights?'

'Yes.'

By later standards of advocacy that might be regarded as a trick question. There was a pointed inversion of the days to catch the unwary witness off his guard. More was to be heard of it. It was the foundation for a later question.

'Did you know that on the Wednesday morning Roberts had accompanied Dimmock home?'

'Yes.'

'Did he tell you that in the course of a conversation?'

'Yes.'

'Was that not a curious conversation to hold with a man you had known for only three days?'

'He did not say that; he merely said he had been with her.'

'For three nights?'

'No.' The witness had seen his mistake.

With the Sunday inverted Clarke thought he had admitted

that he knew Roberts was with the girl Monday, Tuesday and Wednesday – the night of the murder. He was trying to recover himself, in which event all Marshall Hall's spadework would come to nought.

'Why!' exclaimed Marshall. 'I put the three nights to you specifically. I know I did, because I put three nights in the wrong order purposely to mark the question.'

'I did not understand.'

'No. Nor did I,' interposed the Judge. All the advocate's natural excesses of indignation gave vent to themselves.

'I am positive I did. I am as sure as I am standing here. I appeal to the shorthand notes.'

As the shorthand writer laboriously turned to his earlier notes, a pronounced stillness fell upon the court. He found the place, and confirmed Marshall Hall's version.

'Very well,' said the Judge. 'If he misunderstood you, so did I.'

'But,' the KC was not going to allow his carefully laid plan – which had in fact succeeded – to be put aside with that degree of ease, 'I mentioned the three nights.'

'There is no need to get excited, Mr Hall. I did not follow you either.'

Marshall Hall stood silently, as if contemplating his next question, his eyes fixed steadfastly on the jury.

He returned to the witness:

'Do you base the truth of your evidence on the statement that I did not ask you about those three nights?'

'Yes,' came the answer.

Marshall Hall pulled down his seat, and with a flourish of his gown sat down. 'Then I will never so much as ask you another question.' The atmosphere had been electric, but it must be questionable whether the final gesture had any effect on the jury. Juries like fearless advocates and it has been said that the art of cross-examination sometimes lies in the questions omitted rather than in those asked, but since the form of question had muddled not only the witness but the Judge, and possibly the jury as well, it all seemed a trifle pointless.

The cinema, the novel and the theatre have created the

impression in the mind of the layman that every moment in a murder trial is one of breath-taking excitement. Nothing is further from the truth. There are moments of intense boredom, coughing becomes rampant, and even the accused, over whom the struggle is fought, finds himself nodding with ennui. The next four witnesses created much this atmosphere. There was Mrs Lesage to prove, although she hardly did so with any certainty, that her lodgers Roberts, the ship's cook, and Clarke, his new-found friend, had returned home on the Wednesday. It was to be Marshall Hall's comment that the prosecution were trying to prove Wood guilty by calling evidence to show that so many other people could not have committed the murder, although some of his own cross-examination seemed, at times, to be proceeding in the same direction: Mrs Lesage, for example, said she remembered Roberts and Clarke coming home one night at 12.30 o'clock during September; Marshall Hall rose and protested that he had no idea why she was called. Then came Detective Sergeant Osborne to produce the burned fragments of paper which he had found and Sergeant Page to produce the letter from the accommodation address, posted by Wood in conjunction with his brother Charles against the possibility of Robert Wood's connection becoming known. Sergeant Page said that when he went to Phyllis's room on the morning of the discovery of the body, the postcard album was lying on the chair. Marshall Hall pointed out that Shaw had found it on the sewing machine, and that unless one of them was mistaken it must have been moved. Then Sergeant Milton accounted for his failure to find the postcard in the drawer when he searched for it.

The monotony of the preceding evidence and the stuffiness of the atmosphere had induced a state of apathy when Sir Charles Mathews called Robert MacCowan. The witness told the jury how he had been in St Paul's Road on his way to meet his friend Coleman so that both of them might seek work. He described the noise he had heard and the man walking away towards King's Cross Road.

'Can you fix the time?'

'Yes, about twelve minutes to five.'

'Why?'

'I was booked for a job in Brewery Road at five minutes past five.' MacCowan said he had returned to St Paul's Road at a later date and decided that it was No. 29 the man had left and he had picked out the accused at an identification parade. The prosecutor sat down, the witness remained standing – waiting for Marshall Hall to begin. The court came back to life.

'Mr MacCowan,' he began, 'you have said that Coleman, for whom you were calling, was in the habit of leaving a light burning in his room to show that he was coming.'

'Yes.'

'And also that when you heard the noise behind you, you thought it was Coleman?'

'Yes, that's right.'

'On this particular night, was there a light in his room?'

'Yes.'

'Then why did you think he was following you?'

The witness was in his first turmoil. 'Well, when I met him at the gates in Brewery Road he told me he had taken his wife a cup of tea and then left leaving the light burning.'

'But, Mr MacCowan,' with a sidelong glance at the jury to ensure they were listening, 'at the time you passed No. 29 you did not know of this. You must have thought that he was still at home. Therefore he could not have been in the gateway?'

'He had told me that before,' said the witness weakly.

Marshall Hall turned to other fields. 'Before the magistrate you said it was five minutes to five when the man left the gate?'

'Yes, and I stand by that now.'

The plain-clothes officer had said the lamps were extinguished at twenty-three minutes to five, so Marshall Hall was still on safe ground.

'Do you now say it was twelve minutes to five?'

'Yes. I walked the distance and found out I was wrong since that morning. Going by my clock at home I put the time at twelve minutes to five.'

'Have you altered the statement, because before the magistrate you were cross-examined as to when the street lights were out?'

'No. I had not timed myself in walking the distance.'

Then followed a series of short, quickly phrased questions.

'Were the standard lights out?'

'No, I am certain they were on.'

'What sort of morning was it?'

'It was drizzly, thick, muggy.'

'Do you know that not a drop of rain fell in London that day?'

'I call weather like that when there is dew, muggy,' gulped the witness. 'I've not swallowed a dictionary. I'm Suffolk. That's how we talk in Suffolk.'

'In Suffolk a morning not raining is drizzly?'

'Yes.'

'Now, did you tell Sergeant Ball that you saw the man coming down the steps of No. 29?'

'Yes. When we go to make a statement we are not so "fly" as when we come to be cross-examined. I was not so particular – I did not listen particularly to what was being read over to me.'

Marshall Hall exploded again.

'Not so "fly"? Do you mean to say that knowing that a man's life might depend on your description, you did not take particular note of what the Sergeant read over to you?'

'I said I saw a man's back.'

'Have you no regard for human life?'

'Yes, or I shouldn't have come to give evidence. One life's as good as another.' It would have seemed that in the eyes of the witness Wood was guilty before he had been tried.

'Is that how you behave in Suffolk?'

'Yes, that is.'

He was next cross-examined closely about the type of coat the man was wearing and his general description.

'Would you describe the man as broad-shouldered?'

'He has broader shoulders than I have.'

Hall pushed back his wig and roared across the Court in disgust, 'Would you describe a bluebottle as an elephant because it is bigger than a fly?' A murmur rippled through the Court, but the KC paid no heed and relentlessly pursued the cross-examination.

The only question put by Sir Charles, when he re-examined, caused MacCowan to agree that there was an electric light thirty-six yards from No. 29 and another one twenty-three yards away in the opposite direction.

With the Judge's permission Marshall Hall was allowed to put further questions in cross-examination, based, no doubt, on something he had seen in MacCowan's original written statement which he had omitted to put to him earlier.

'Was there a police constable on the opposite side of the road?' he asked MacCowan.

'Yes,' he replied.

It was time for lunch and a special edition of the newspapers. It was some while before MacCowan was to be spared from further agonies in the witness box, but after he had been interrogated about the identification parade he was allowed to rest. His evidence and ordeal were at an end. The case was by now disclosing the most outrageous conduct. Everyone concerned was receiving abusive and threatening letters. Someone had chalked 'blood money' over MacCowan's doors, and before he left the Court MacCowan protested to the Judge, '. . . anyone would think I did the murder. If I saw, with my own eyes, a man getting his throat cut in the street, I don't think I would give evidence again.' The Judge commiserated, adding he would deal harshly with anyone found indulging in such practice as intimidating witnesses, but it was self-evident that MacCowan's cross-examination had given him some unhappy moments, and his protest was a two-pronged gesture; a protest against the despoiler of doors and against Marshall Hall, as a despoiler of characters.

In the afternoon Inspector Neil outlined the course of the investigations, leaving Marshall Hall little of importance on which to cross-examine, and the trial reached the end of its second day. Wood sat silently and imperturbably through the proceedings. At one stage a noted alienist, who was in court, turned to his companion and said, 'Why look, I do believe he's sketching the Judge.' Indeed he was, and continued doing so until a horrified warder told him it was not permitted.

The first witness, on the third day of the trial, was John P. Mair, who gave evidence that the mysterious Scotch Bob, whose name proved to be Mackie, was with him in Scotland on

11 September and that he could not have been in St Paul's Road. But it was the attempt to prove this alibi for Scotch Bob which gave rise to a mild sensation after he had been called into Court to be identified. Mair had produced a document which, he asserted, enabled him to fix the date when Mackie was in Scotland last as 15 September. Marshall Hall noticed something about the document.

'The document which you have produced, signed by Mackie, bears two dates, Mr Mair, 15.9.07 and 15.8.07?'

'Mackie must have made a mistake in the date,' was the answer.

'You have no desire to help this man, I suppose?'

'Certainly not.'

'And you say he was in your employment on 11 September?'

'He was.'

'How do you know that you saw Mackie at the hotel in Scotland on the night of 11 September?'

'From documents I have at the hotel.'

It again seems strange that Marshall Hall made so little of the two dates. If the mistaken date was 15.9.07, the alibi would have been exploded. Yet he did not pursue it, although there was evidence that Scotch Bob had threatened the deceased.

Mair was followed into the box by Sergeant Ball, who was cross-examined with some degree of thoroughness about the statement which MacCowan had made to him.

'MacCowan says that when you read it over to him he did not take any particular notice. Did you read it so that he could hear all that you said?'

'Certainly. He made one or two corrections.'

William Moss, the principal designer of Wood's employers, next told the Court of his conversation about 'the unfortunate woman' being murdered, of his belief that the man who wrote the postcard could draw, to which Wood had replied, 'I think he can.' In answer to Marshall Hall, he said that Wood bore an exceptionally good character and that he had seen no peculiarity in his gait. In re-examination Sir Charles pressed him to the uttermost to acknowledge some unusual features in Wood's walk, without success. Indeed, so far did Sir Charles Mathews press him that Marshall Hall was constrained to protest that he must not cross-examine his own witnesses. 'Oh! I don't mind,' replied the obliging Mr Moss. The Judge, however, was a man of strong views. He had from time to time indicated his disapproval of the happenings the case disclosed and, when both counsel had finished, he embarked on a line of interrogation of his own.

'You thought him a high-minded man in the works. Had you any idea of the immoral life you have now heard the accused was leading?'

'No. I did not think that he held any puritanical views of life, but that there was anything out of the normal, I was unaware.'

'I do not quite know what your answer means. Had you any idea he was leading an immoral life?'

'No.'

'It is, I believe, admitted, that though nominally living under the protection of Shaw, this woman was receiving men. Had you any idea that Wood was living with such a woman?'

'No.'

'You know he admits writing the postcard?'

'Yes.'

These questions were clearly designed to discredit the witness's character reference for Wood, a course which the prosecution had not seen fit to pursue. Marshall Hall was not prepared to permit this for a moment. The best of Marshall Hall manifested itself. The man who abhorred unfairness and any hint of injustice was on his feet with no slow, measured rise. It was the spring of a tiger.

'I do not understand your lordship's question,' he said. Perhaps less notice would have been taken of such an observation from another silk. It was an interjection made without rudeness, but he had a reputation for pugnacity and this was manifestly in the Judge's mind when he answered.

'Are you addressing me or the jury? If you are speaking to me, I wish you would not look at the jury – I am taking the accused's own statement.' Ignoring the interruption, the Judge returned to the witness. 'Had you any idea he was living with such a woman as that—'

He had no answer. Hall was up again.

'There is not a tittle of evidence—'

'I am addressing a witness,' Mr Justice Grantham was now also ruffled. 'Counsel must not interrupt when I am putting questions on the evidence in the interests of justice. I must ask you not to argue with me. I shall permit no argument as to the way in which I am putting my questions to him.'

Hall recovered himself, glanced towards the jury and said, 'With great deference, I only wish, also in the interests of justice, to point out that there is not a particle of evidence that the accused ever stayed with the woman, or had improper relations with her' – and certainly, it may be added, no evidence that he was 'living' with her. Not merely was his observation correct but his interruption achieved its purpose. The matter lapsed and the witness gave no answer.

It was typical of Marshall Hall when in fighting trim. It is a wise precaution when arguing with authority to ensure that you are in the right. Here he was on safe ground.

The witness left the box to make way for Lambert, Wood's former colleague, who had been invited by Wood to support his false alibi. He gave evidence of meeting with Wood on the Wednesday at the Eagle; Miss Raven, the barmaid, confirmed his evidence.

Interest lagged until the ladies in court leaned forward to see in what it was that the men were showing such interest. Ruby Young was walking to the witness box. The public were unsure how to take Ruby. For some she was a Delilah who had delivered her lover into the hands of the Philistines; to others she was a discarded sweetheart, cast aside when no longer needed, and called back to office when expediency required, to defame her name and reputation for her one-time lover. True, by the standards of 1907, she had little reputation to lose, but the more that can be said against a woman, the less she wants to talk about it. Her wishes were of little account as she was taken, in detail, through the whole story from her first meeting with Robert Wood, to the night she spent, whispering, in the room adjoining his father's bedroom, down to the last meeting when at the instigation of the police she had brought her one-time fiancé within the grasping arms of the law. At one point she turned her back to the Court and wept silently for several minutes while the Judge sat examining the 'Rising Sun' postcard. She had been in the witness box a considerable time before Sir Charles Mathews brought her to the concluding line of her piece. 'You have walked with the prisoner a good deal in your friendship and have sometimes walked beside him?'

'Yes.'

'Have you noticed anything peculiar about him?'

'Yes. He had a walk no one else could copy.'

'What is that peculiarity?'

'He walked with his left hand in his pocket and brought the right shoulder forward.'

Marshall Hall began his cross-examination quietly, the bullying manner put aside.

'Is it the case that you did not say anything about the peculiarity in the accused's walk until 4 December?'

'Yes. That was when I was first asked.'

'Did you say that the prisoner was of a kind and lovable disposition and that you had formed a great affection for him?'

'Yes.'

'What was the first thing you remember saying to the accused about this murder?'

'I said, "If you will go to Scotland Yard and tell how you sent the postcard you will be free".'

'Therefore you could not have believed that he committed the murder?'

'No, I could not.'

'Have you written a letter to the *News of the World* saying that you were not in any way instigated by the reward of £100 in making the statement to the police?'

'Yes.'

'And to the effect that you would not accept it?'

'Yes.'

Then came the most vital phrases in the whole of the trial.

'With regard to the arrangement which you had come to, was it that you should say that the accused was in your company on the night of Wednesday, 11 September, from 6.30 to 10.30. Is that correct?'

'Yes, it is.'

'Has it ever occurred to you that, having regard to Dr Thompson's evidence, that would be a useless alibi for the murder, but a perfect alibi for the meeting of the girl? Dr Thompson's evidence is that the girl must have died between three and four o'clock on the early morning of 12 September?'

'It did not strike me that it was a useless alibi then.'

Here was the crux of Wood's defence. The murder was said to have occurred in the early morning. For what reason would the assailant, who must have known the time when he committed the murder, be manufacturing an alibi for some totally different time? Did it not indicate that Wood did not know the time the murder was committed and therefore that he could not possibly be the assailant? Was it not clear that Wood's anxiety was to cover something else? And was it not to hide his association with prostitutes – common strumpets as they were called in those days – rather than any guilty participation in the gruesome crime? Although really a matter of argument, interposed as it was in the evidence of Ruby Young in the form of question and answer it had a far greater effect on the jury. But could it save the accused? Or would the sheer weight of the remaining evidence outweigh the value of this vital question? The Court adjourned; the third day of the trial of *R.* v. *Wood* had concluded.

It is odd that Marshall Hall referred to Dr Thompson's evidence as being that the girl had died between three and four o'clock in the morning. His evidence was that he saw the body shortly after 1 p.m. on the Wednesday and that she had been dead seven or eight hours. He also said death was instantaneous which put the time of assault and death at between five and six o'clock in the morning. Moreover, that timing made the making of an alibi for 6.30 to 10.30 on the previous evening even more telling in Wood's interest.

The intervening week-end, during which the jury visited the scene of the crime and the surrounding neighbourhood, enabled the Sunday papers to make the most of the trial, and when Monday arrived, and the fourth day of the case was due to open, the crowd seeking admission to the galleries was larger than ever. Exactly what draws spectators to a murder trial? Perhaps a combination of many things; a sense of the dramatic, a sadistic desire to see others suffer, a wish to observe the arts of the advocate and a famous one at that, an interest in criminology, and, perhaps more frequently, to take some part, however small, in a sensational happening that will enable the spectator to become the authority in the matter to less fortunate acquaintances. None of these factors pay heed to the feelings of the accused, his relatives and friends; in some cases, the surging crowds, avidly leaning forward to gather every detail of the wretched man's misfortunes, can occasion great pain to the prisoner in the dock and to his family, but it did not seem so in the case of Robert Wood. Throughout he maintained an imperturbable air, as if witnessing a struggle for another's life rather than his own. Where others might have wept, he sketched; where others might have cringed, he sat unbended and unmoved.

After Mr Tinkham, the fellow workman of the accused, had told of his conversation about the facsimile of Wood's writing in the paper, and of his promise to Wood that because of his father's illness he would make no disclosure, Mrs Emily Lawrence was called to take the oath.

'Did you ever see the accused and Dimmock together?' asked Mr Bodkin, the junior counsel.

'Yes,' she replied. 'About fifteen months ago I first saw them in conversation in the Pindar of Wakefield public house, Gray's Inn Road.'

Throughout her evidence she repeatedly looked towards Wood with an expression which seemed to convey a mixture of malice and disdain.

Step by step, she was brought to 9 September; she described the drink she and Mrs Smith had had with Wood and Mrs Smith's remark that Phyllis would be jealous. 'Dimmock and the accused then left,' she continued, 'the girl saying they were going to the Holborn Empire.'

'What happened then?'

'I noticed that the girl did not seem to want to go with the accused. She appeared to have to go.'

'Why do you say that?'

'She passed some uncomplimentary remarks about him. She seemed very nervous of him.'

Counsel resumed his place.

'Is Mrs Florence Smith a friend of yours?' was Marshall Hall's first question to the 'reformed' Emily Lawrence.

'Yes.'

'Did you say before the magistrate that she, Dimmock and yourself followed the same calling?'

'No.'

'What were you doing at the public house?'

'I was there for a bit of recreation.'

'Did you lead the same life as Dimmock many years ago?'

'Before I was married. Five or six years back.'

'Was she not of the lowest type of prostitute?'

Emily was on the defensive. 'No, she was not.' Indignation swept over her face.

'What was your impression of the deceased?'

'She was a very nice, respectable, clean and tidy girl,' she replied with emphasis.

'As good as any in Euston Road.'

'Yes.'

Marshall questioned her on her ability to recognise the accused. 'In one place you said you saw Wood at 8.30 o'clock on the Monday, and at another you said 6.30?'

'Wood was with Dimmock when she first went into the house. She went out and came back, and he was still there.'

'Do you swear that you were there all the time?'

'It might have been later than 6.30 when I went there the first time.'

'Why did you go there?'

'To meet Mrs Smith.' The indignation surged again. 'You are trying to make me a bad character,' added the reformed Emily.

'God forbid that I should make you one. What was the origin of your feeling against the accused?'

'I have no feeling against him.'

'Oh yes you have.'

'I tell you I have not. I simply came here to speak the truth in the interests of justice.'

Marshall Hall looked at the jury.

'Then, why have you been looking at the prisoner as you have done, while you have been giving evidence?'

'Good gracious' – a mild remark from the reformed Emily, no doubt – 'aren't me eyes me own to look around with?' Momentarily she lost her composure.

'Now what is it? I am using my eyes too. What have you got against him?'

'Nothing. I'm here to speak the truth.'

True or otherwise, her evidence was concluded. The witness box was taken by Mrs Smith in confirmation of the evidence of Emily Lawrence. The next lady in the procession to the witness box was Gladys Warren. Bodkin examined her as to her relation with Phyllis, asking whether she knew the accused.

'When did you first get to know him?'

'When Dimmock stayed with me at Judd Street in 1906. I only knew him by sight. He was in the Rising Sun with Dimmock. I have seen him twice since that.' She added that Wood had known Dimmock for much longer than he admitted. Marshall Hall decided not to press her unduly, and the short nature of his cross-examination left the impression this part of the allegations was not being challenged by Wood.

Along the narrow passageway dividing the dock from the public seats came a jaunty, self-assured figure. The afternoon was drawing into evening; the light was darkening around the glass roof; the electric lights were burning; that drowsy, musty, yet fascinating smell which permeates a court room in the late afternoon was perceptible to the nostrils; two uninteresting witnesses on trifling matters had lulled the onlookers back to a state bordering apathy, and the advent of the well-proportioned gentleman entering the box raised hopes of something brighter. Sir Charles Mathews rose to examine. The air of the witness had something of self-confidence mixed with a determination not to be bothered by the surroundings. Not, perhaps, without reason. He might not pay for the upkeep of the Central Criminal Court, but he was one of the unhappy band who provided work, without which the participants in its daily business would be unemployed.

'What is your full name?'

'My name's John William Crabtree.'

'What is your present address?'

'I have no fixed abode.'

It had only recently become unfixed, it might be observed.

'When did you first see the accused?'

'In May 1906, he visited the house at 1 Bidborough Street, where Dimmock was living as my tenant.'

'Were the people who lived there respectable?'

Crabtree screwed up his face. In Bidborough Street respectability was a relative term. 'Well,' he replied, 'one of 'em was a railway porter.'

'Can you remember any particular occasion when the accused was there?'

'Yes, I can. On one occasion the accused and the deceased were together in 'er room. Dimmock called me up. She had a sheet round her. She asked me to pawn a cigarette case with a monogram on it.' Crabtree paused and pushed his hands into the tops of his trousers. 'I asked who it belonged to. Wood said it was his. I questioned him about it, and then he said not to bother about pawning it.' He waited and, with a knowing glance towards the jury, added in confidential tone, 'I refused to take it to the pawnshop though.'

'Did you ever see Wood after that?'

'Yes, about 11 June 1906. One evening Dimmock was away at Portsmouth with Biddle. Wood came around making enquiries for her. I told him she was at Portsmouth. She came back – a Saturday it was – ten-thirty in the morning. Wood was in the house by eight o'clock in the evening.'

When, ultimately, Marshall Hall came to his feet he was concerned to place the unreliability of Crabtree beyond the jury's doubt.

'You have had two terms of imprisonment for keeping a disorderly house?'

'Yes. I was discharged from prison ten days ago.'

'So that for the last twelve to fifteen months you have been in prison practically the whole time?'

'Yes.'

'What was the first thing you went to prison for?'

'That's got nuffin' to do with this case.' Crabtree knew his rights, he did.

'You are going to answer my question. Turn round, man, so that the jury can see you. Now – what was it?'

'Street stealing.' It was a most terrible confession for a man of Crabtree's standing in his profession.

'When was that?'

'Four or five years ago.'

'And you also went to three years' penal servitude for horse stealing?'

'Yes.'

'Do you ever tell the truth?'

'Yes. I try to.'

'Do you always succeed in doing what you try to do?'

'Not always,' replied Crabtree with a grin at the jury.

'Will you not treat this matter with levity?'

'Well, you're trying to make fun of me.'

'Did you ever try to live an honest life?'

'Yes.'

'Did you fail at it?'

'Yes.' Another grin. 'I have lived for fifty-six years and I've only been in jug three times.'

'Has anyone ever enquired into your mental condition?'

'Not that I'm aware of.'

'Are you sober now?'

'I'm sober all right. I've never tasted licker in me life.'

'Do you swear that you saw Wood in one of the houses you kept?'

'Yes, emphatically, on me oath and without a shadder of daht.'

'How did the police know about this?' Crabtree shrugged his shoulders with an impatient gesture. 'You'd better ask 'em. They came and took me out of my cell and frightened the life out of me. At first I thought they wanted me for the murder.'

'What? How did you know the murdered woman was the one who lived in your house?'

'I only knew what the police told me.'

'Did you give the police a description of a man named Scottie – a motor driver?'

'Yes, I did.'

'Is this the description?' Marshall Hall read out the details. Crabtree listened but began nodding his head violently.

'Aw,' he said pointing at the paper, 'that's Scottie, that ain't Scotch Bob.'

'Then they have got the wrong "Scotch" one?'

'He's not the Scottie I mean.'

'Did you say in your statement that Scottie had threatened her with a razor?'

'Yes.'

'Did you inform the superintendent of the block of flats where Dimmock once stayed of her character, your object being to get back certain furniture from her?'

'Yes.'

'And did you also make Shaw, with whom the girl lived, pay money?'

'Yes.'

'Was there also another man who was friendly with her and lived with her?' This question was curiously phrased, by introducing the word 'also', in view of Marshall Hall's earlier outburst when he told the Judge there was no evidence that the accused had ever lived with her – as was the fact.

'Yes.'

'Did your wife point out that man in Euston Road?'

'Yes.'

'By that man do you mean the accused?'

'Yes.'

'When the police first came to see you were you frightened?'

'Yes.'

'How did the police come to ask you about the murder?'

'That's a question the police ought to answer. I don't know what brought them there. They took me out of a cell.'

'Did you think they were going to charge you with the murder?'

'Yes.'

'How did you know that she had been murdered?'

'I didn't know till they told me. They do it in a rahndabaht way. You know the police don't tell the truth.'

'Is that your experience of the police?'

'Yes, it is.' Crabtree looked round the Court, threw back his shoulders, leaned forward, snapped his fingers and murmured, 'I don't care *that* for the police.' His evidence was finished. A short re-examination by Sir Charles Mathews and he walked back along the aisle between the seats and dock, out the way he had come, the same jaunty walk indicating the self-same air of condescension. Nothing remained to the prosecution but to call Alexander Mackie to say he was known as Scotch Bob and had been in Scotland. When Mackie left the box, Sir Charles turned to the Judge and said, 'M'lord, that is the case on the part of the prosecution.' The evidence was completed. It was the turn of the defence.

Chapter X

A high degree of proof is required on a charge of murder, and it is presumed, until the contrary is proved, that an accused person is innocent. The prosecution had produced no evidence that Wood was actually on the premises of No. 29 St Paul's Road on the night of 11 September 1907; the evidence of identity, particularly in respect of MacCowan, related to a time and condition which made certainty of identification questionable; and there had been no suggestion of any motive for the crime. A motive is not a *sine qua non* to a conviction for murder, but the absence of one must remain a vital matter for consideration when deciding if the crime was likely to have been committed by the man in the dock. As against this, there were many serious points which indicated that Wood may have been the murderer, and Marshall Hall's submission, which he made to the Judge, that the case should proceed no further was not one he could seriously have believed would have been accepted. There was clearly enough to connect the accused with the dead woman on the night of her death to justify leaving the case to the jury. Much would depend, therefore, on the demeanour of the prisoner in the witness box, and on his ability to sustain his story under cross-examination.

Marshall Hall opened the defence to the jury, in the knowledge that it was better for him to anticipate the prosecution's cross-examination of his client by conceding that he had lied and had concocted a false alibi. 'If the accused is not called to give evidence on his own behalf, juries are apt to draw inferences which may well be totally unfounded. We will put that man in the witness box; but he will go into the witness box tomorrow morning – tainted. He will enter it tainted with the fact that he had made statements which are untrue.' He dealt with the evidence he intended to call before coming to the time when Wood was said to have left St Paul's Road. 'Wood is alleged to have left the house a few minutes before five in the morning. Is it credible that any man of the prisoner's temperament could have committed such a crime? Is it credible that after midnight, the accused would creep from his father's home, getting into the woman's house and with some sharp instrument do her to death? Then wait until five minutes to five for no apparent reason, before walking out of the house and back to his home, and an hour or two later to work – calm and collected? Is it credible, I ask?'

Marshall Hall had a magical effect with juries. They hung upon every word as the advocate fought for the life of his wretched client in the dock.

'But if you assume the accused's innocence then everything becomes clear. . . . Seeing the possibility of ruin to his own reputation, and injury to his father's health if he were known to have been associating with women of the deceased's class, the accused did what many other foolish and silly people have done before. He thought it would be better to tell a lie than the truth; so he told a lie. He asked his sweetheart to save him – not to prove that he did not commit the murder, but to prevent his being inculpated in association with a woman who was a low harlot. . . . The murder must have been committed, according to the medical evidence, about three o'clock in the morning. [Once again Marshall Hall seems, incredibly enough, to have got the wrong time of death.] The alibi was valuable only for proving that the accused was not with Dimmock in the bar of the Eagle, Camden Town on the night of 11 September.'

He continued, expounding Orr's theory as to why Roberts had contacted May Campbell, supported as it was now by Roberts's admission that he had spoken to her and knew her. He turned to MacCowan's evidence of Wood's departure from No. 29. 'Are you to think that a murderer coming out of a house where he had just left the body of his victim would select a moment to come out when another man's footsteps were clattering along the pavement and a policeman was opposite in the full glare of the electric light, if MacCowan's own account is to be believed?' It is not possible to convey the deep impression which rhetoric such as this can have, and doubtless did have, on a jury. As he described the feet 'clattering along the pavement' it virtually gave life to the words. He continued: 'Statements have been handed to me by the prosecution, of men named Sharples and Harvey, that they saw the woman at 12.30 in company with a man who was not the accused. The only complaint I have to make against the prosecution is that they did not call those witnesses.' Perhaps the jury were unable to appreciate the significance of this complaint. It is the duty of the prosecution to make available all the relevant evidence which comes to its hand in the course of its investigation. They can decide whether or not a witness shall be called but they also have a duty to assist the pursuit of justice and, if the defence request, they should generally be willing (although not bound) to tender witnesses whom the defence wish to cross-examine. The difficulty is that the defence, if left to call the witnesses themselves, may not cross-examine them but must accept the unled evidence which they give. The fact that they may be favourable to the accused is of no account, for the prosecution must strive, not for a conviction, but for justice. Marshall went on: 'If the Crown condescends to call a man like Crabtree, why not call those men? No words can express the contempt and horror I feel for a man like Crabtree. It is a criticism of the weakness of the case for the prosecution that they should have had to call a witness like Crabtree.'

However, it has been questioned how accurate this complaint was in substance. A certain famous judge once said, 'If a man without request blacks my boots, what can I do but put them on?' It may similarly be asked, if Wood chose to associate with people of the same class as Crabtree what could the prosecution do but call them? That it was a double-edged proposition seemed to pass unnoticed in the intensity of the argument.

Marshall Hall was reaching his peroration. 'Gentlemen, in the last three days you may have thought that, now and then,

I was pressing a witness unfairly, that I urged an unfair advantage, that I asked an unworthy question. If I seemed to exceed the proper limits, I implore you to forgive me. My whole anxiety was for my client. Gentlemen, his life is at stake. I cannot rob the witnesses of the prosecution of that. They have far less to lose at my hands than he at yours. This burden has been lying very heavily on my shoulders. It will pass to yours, all too soon.' There was a scuffle in the witness box and a member of the jury fainted. It was not surprising. An onlooker described his effort as 'passionate and pulverising rhetoric which reduced the jury to a state of pulp'.

The following morning he called George Wood, the father of the accused. He gave his evidence in a forthright, open manner; told of the breaking of the bottle of linament and how that enabled him to fix the Wednesday; explained that the interconnection of events convinced him that it was that night when his son came home and said that he had breakfast with him next morning. 'Did the police come and ask for your son's overcoat?' asked Marshall Hall.

'Yes! And they started to search for something.'

'What did you do?'

'I said that I might save them trouble as I had examined the drawers the night before. One said, "We're lookin' for something else now" and put his hand up the chimney.'

'What did he find there?'

'Soot.'

He went on to assert that his son was not wearing his coat about that time and to describe the injuries to his hand which made him carry his left hand in his pocket.

'Has he any marked peculiarity of walk?'

'He has no peculiarity of walk. He's a real neat walker.'

It has been well said that the truthful witness has nothing to fear from the most skilful cross-examination and Sir Charles Mathews could make little headway with old George Wood.

'On the night of 4 October did Inspector Neil interrogate you about your son's movements on the night of 11 September?'

'Yes.'

'Did you tell the Inspector that your son would return from business and then go out again; and that you could not say at what time he would return?'

'Oh, yes, very likely.'

'Did you go on to say that as a rule he put his head into your room and said "Good night", but that you could not speak of any particular night?'

'I do not recollect that.'

'Did you not admit saying that before the coroner?'

'I cannot recollect.'

'You may have said so?'

'I don't think it at all possible.'

'Is that as far as you'd like to go?'

'Yes.'

They passed to the spilled linament.

'When did you go to purchase some more linament?'

'On the following Monday.'

'Why not before?'

'Because I had not spilled it before.'

'Why did you not say that at the police court?'

'Because they did not ask me.'

The stepbrother and Charles Wood were the next to be called, the former to corroborate the father's story; the latter to describe the incidents connected with the letter at the poste restante. Then a representative of the Electric Light Company to prove that the lights were extinguished between 4.37 and 4.41 on the morning of 12 September. As this witness disappeared out of the Court, a well-built man made his entrance. He strode into the box and took the oath in a determined fashion; he was the 'most important piece of information which ... may turn the whole course of events' about which Newton had written to Hall on the very eve of the trial.

'Is your full name William Westcott?'

'It is.'

'You're a ticket collector at King's Cross Station?'

'I am.'

'Where do you live?'

'At 26 St Paul's Road.'

'Where is that in relation to No. 29?'

'It's on the opposite side of the road, about 250 yards away.'

'What time do you go to work?'

'At five minutes to five in the morning.'

'What time did you leave home on 12 September?'

'I would have left home at five to five. I was on the early shift.'

'Did you see anyone?'

'I saw a man going in the direction of Brewery Road. I keep chickens at the back and was suspicious.'

'Could you identify him?'

'No.'

'Have you an unusual walk?'

'Yes, I'm a boxer. I have a swing in my walk. Especially in the morning, as I have been told that a swing of the arm is good for the chest.'

'How were you dressed?'

'I had my collar turned up. Like this.' The witness turned up his collar, threw out his chest and engaged in a jaunty walk up and down the witness box.

Sir Charles cross-examined.

'Is this not rather late to come forward?'

'I don't know.'

'Why did you not come forward before?'

'I cannot say.'

'Did you make a statement to the defence on 15 December?'

'Yes.'

'On your way to work you would not pass No. 29, but you would go in the opposite direction?'

'That's correct.'

In re-examination Marshall Hall asked only whether the witness had mentioned his presence in St Paul's Road to a photographer who had told him to communicate with the defence. The witness replied, 'Yes,' and with his chest out, giving full play to his jaunty walk, he marched out of the court.

Was this the man whom MacCowan had seen? That the man he saw came from No. 29 was only ascertained by him on a subsequent visit to St Paul's Road. Might it not have been Westcott whom he saw, and might it not have been another house in the road? Memory plays surprising tricks. Marshall

Hall offered to call sixty-five persons from the place where the accused worked to prove that Wood had no peculiarity in his walk. To begin with he contented himself with calling one, and, having heard him, the prosecutor, to save time, expressed himself satisfied that the others would say the same as he. Then the defence called the angler who saw Wood returning home at midnight while he was looking for worms, and after him the two witnesses whom the prosecution had discovered but failed to call: Sharples and Harvey. They said they were in the Euston Road the night of 11 September and had seen Dimmock with a big, well-built man, who was not the accused.

Marshall Hall gathered his papers together, took the piece of pink tape from around them between his fingers, and in a commanding voice announced, 'I call the prisoner Robert Wood.'

Every head turned in the direction of the prisoner: the first prisoner charged with murder in England to volunteer to enter the witness box and submit to cross-examination; the first person so charged who had dared to do so in the nine years that the course had been open to accused persons. He pushed back the chair and walked steadily to the side of the dock; the warder opened the door leading into the Court and he stepped towards the witness box. He was the target of every pair of eyes and all were looking at one thing: his walk. As he strode smartly between the packed Court benches, he carried his left hand in his pocket. On the way, he passed his father, who was sitting in the Court. He smiled at him and with a light manner said, 'Well, Dad, cheer up.' The conduct of this man in the witness box would literally spell the difference between life and death. One false move and he might plunge irrevocably to his doom; a straight, frank, and honest dealing with questions and he could leave the Court a free man. This was the crucial moment. This would decide all. What was it to be? The atmosphere was electric, a silence of great expectancy hung over the court. Even the Judge followed the movements of the witness with unusual interest. He took the oath in a loud clear voice, and Marshall Hall began. First his description and then, 'Did you kill Emily Dimmock?'

There was no reply.

'Wood, did you kill Emily Dimmock?'

'It is ridiculous.' It was the sort of answer that would chill an advocate's blood.

'You must answer straight,' urged Marshall. 'I will only ask you straight questions. Did you kill her?'

'No, I did not.'

'When did you first become acquainted with Dimmock?'

'Friday, 6 September.'

'That is true?'

'Perfectly true.'

'Do you emphatically deny Crabtree's evidence?'

'Yes.'

'Were you ever in a house of his?' The desire of the witness to engage in histrionics reasserted itself, to the concern of Marshall Hall.

'No. I hope God will destroy me this moment if I have ever entered a house of his or knew him.'

'Wood,' said Marshall Hall, 'I know you are under the stress of a great emotion but try to keep to the questions. How did you come to know Dimmock?'

'It was on 6 September in the Rising Sun, under the glare of the light. I will leave that to the jury. No doubt many of the jury will know what goes on in public houses,' he said, turning to the jury. He was behaving like the lead in a third-rate melodrama rather than as a man overawed by the enormity of the struggle for his life. Would the jury think he was putting on an act and would he antagonise them?

'You must address your replies to me and not to the jury.' Marshall Hall's tone was becoming less kind as the witness disregarded his advice. 'Did she speak to you?'

'She asked for a penny for the automatic gramophone.' It was unlikely that Wood would make mistakes in the next part of his evidence, he had told it so often. First to Tinkham, then to his brother; next to the police, to the lawyers, to his father, over and over again he had been through the story and once more he recounted the details to the jury. Only this time it would be the last time. There would be no other opportunity after this. In 1907, there was no Court of Criminal Appeal.

He arrived at 9 September, and denied that he had ever seen Dimmock in the Pindar of Wakefield. He still relapsed into his theatrical and supercilious air of detachment. When Marshall Hall asked him whether the girl had done anything with his sketch book while they were in the Rising Sun, he said she had it on her lap looking at the postcards. But he could not resist adding in parenthesis and in an affected tone, 'In fact, I may say she had some intelligence to appeal to.' He was the kind of witness of whom advocates despair. When he was asked how Phyllis was dressed when she and he met Lambert in the bar of the Eagle, he replied, 'I cannot say. If I were a girl I might be able to tell you.' Which view would the jury take of him? Would they regard him as calm in the knowledge of innocence, or overacting in the quasi-madness of guilt?

'What time did you arrive home on the night of 11 September?'

'At about eleven-thirty or twelve.'

'How long had you been with Phyllis Dimmock that night?'

'I was with her all the evening. I left her at about eleven o'clock in the Eagle public house.'

'What was the first thing you did when you got home?'

'I went straight to my father's room.'

'What for?'

'He had been seriously ill. I also wanted the alarm clock for waking me in the morning.'

'Have you any particular recollection of taking the clock that night?'

'No. But I did it regularly.'

'Did you leave the house again on that Wednesday night?'

'No, I did not.'

'You went to work next morning?'

'Yes.'

Marshall Hall continued to lead him through the events and allegations of the prosecution, down to the meetings with Ruby Young.

'Why did you want Ruby Young to say that she was with you on that Wednesday night, when you were in fact with Emily Dimmock in the Eagle?'

'Is there not a certain amount of disgrace in it?' He wheeled

129

towards the jury again. 'It must appeal to the average man that he would like to steer clear of a thing like that.'

'Did your father know of your relations with Ruby Young?'

'He knew of her and had seen us together.'

'Ruby Young has said that she stayed the night in your father's house. Is that true?'

'That is a lie. She had been to Frederick Street but she had never passed the night there.'

'Wood, it has been said by a police officer that you said to him "If it comes to a crisis I shall have to open out." Is that true?'

'It is untrue; it has hurt me more than anything. It's a hit below the belt, the officer was most friendly towards me.'

Marshall Hall handed to Wood the burned fragment of the letter found in the grate of St Paul's Road. He slowly read such parts as were decipherable and asked the prisoner to check them with him: '... ill ... you ... ar ... of ... the C ... town ... R ... Wednesday ... has ... ill'. He turned the paper over and pointed out the words 'rest', 'excuse', 'good' and 'fond'. Another turn of the paper and the word 'Mon'.

'Now have you carefully considered the matter, Wood, and are you able to give any explanation of that writing?'

'No,' was the reply.

'Can you account for the fragments being found at St Paul's Road?'

'No. The only thing I can suggest is that they were fragments of some little sketches that I was doing in the public house bar.'

His examination-in-chief was concluded. Marshall Hall sat down. It was late in the afternoon, and the Court adjourned until the following day. It was to be an eventful day. It would be the first occasion that a man charged with murder in England had faced the probing questions of a skilled cross-examiner. Tomorrow Wood must fight for his life, with one of the most dexterous, although the most fair, cross-examiners at the Criminal Bar. It was a breath-taking prospect.

'When did your association with Dimmock begin?' asked Sir Charles when he opened his cross-examination the next morning.

'On Friday, 6 September.'

'What sort of an account do you give of the association?'

'It was short, casual and harmless.'

'It was confined from a Friday to the following Wednesday?'

'Yes.'

'Beyond that, had you anything to fear from publicity being given to your association with the woman?' The point of the second question became apparent. If this was a 'short, casual and harmless' association why go to all the trouble of fabricating stories to hide it?

Wood thought for a moment and replied. 'The association was low.'

'Look at the "Rising Sun" postcard. It was written by you. Did you keep the assignation which was made on the face of the postcard?'

'I went to the Rising Sun, but later.'

'Do you suggest that the appointment which you kept was not made by the postcard?' Every question was short, curt and to the point. None brooked of avoidance.

'There was no seriousness attached to it. The words "If you please" explain that it was immaterial to me.'

The prosecutor was not to be outflanked.

'I'm not directing my question to materiality. Did you keep the appointment made on the postcard?' He raised his high-pitched voice and whipped the question from his tongue: 'Yes or No?'

'Not on the Saturday it was intended for, when it was written.' For some minutes the two fought over this issue, Sir Charles suggesting that no one would have written those words on a postcard unless it referred to a definite appointment; the witness arguing that he had no appointment in mind.

'Does that postcard refer to an appointment which you had with Phyllis Dimmock?'

'If I must answer you like that – yes.'

'All those people have said they saw you beckon to Phyllis Dimmock when you went in on the Friday. Do you deny it?'

'I should say so. I cannot understand why the manager of the Rising Sun, who would be most likely to see everything that passed, is not called. Yet he is kept away and the barman, who would see least, is called.'

'Really,' rejoined the cross-examiner. 'If we had known the importance to you we should have brought him.' Then in more severe tones: 'Keep your mind to the evidence.'

Question after question was reeled at the head of the witness. 'Is Mr Sneeth correct in saying that you have been a frequenter at the Rising Sun for some time prior to September this year?'

'It depends on what you mean by "frequenter". I have lived all my life within a stone's throw of the house.'

'Can you pledge yourself to the time you arrived at the Rising Sun on the Monday?'

'No.'

'How long were you in the Rising Sun?'

'Again, I could not say.'

'Was there not an arrangement made between the two women in your hearing to go to the Euston Music Hall, while you and Dimmock went to the Holborn Empire?'

'No.'

'How shall we characterise that? As an exaggeration, or as something which took place out of your hearing?'

'I should say a concoction, I think.'

'Apart from the question of time, where did you go?'

'Beyond that I was in her company at the Rising Sun, I cannot tell anything, some of the folk can tell you exactly what I did. I really do not know.'

'That does not convey much to me, because I am submitting that you are the person who can tell me what you did. Where did you go in that woman's company?'

'I cannot say.'

The novelist Sir Hall Caine, who was watching the cross-examination, was to say, 'Not once or twice but again and again, under the searching light of a withering but always temperate cross-examination, the witness was being destroyed by his anxiety to prove too much, by his overweening personal vanity, by his excess of small cleverness, by his little unnecessary flourishes of personal pride, by his want of logical balance, by his apparent inability to distinguish between the facts that were paramount and dangerous to his chance of life and those that were secondary and only damaging to his reputation'.

The cross-examination went on with unabated fury.

'At what time did you leave the Rising Sun?'

'Such an idle hour is carelessly spent and I could not speak definitely as to the time.' He might have been the matinee idol playing his part in a drawing-room playlet. His air was one of complete aloofness.

The most pregnant portion of the cross-examination was approaching. Every observer in the Court was intently awaiting every word. The Judge leaned forward over his desk, the notabilities were forgotten; they were straining their every nerve to hear the replies. The Court was deadly silent, the air filled with expectation of the next rapier thrust.

'I suggest to you that on the night of the 10th, after putting your head in at the door, you went away and wrote a letter of assignation to Phyllis Dimmock for the night of Wednesday the 11th?'

'I did not.'

'I further suggest to you that, having seen her on the Monday and Tuesday in the Rising Sun with a man, you changed the meeting place to the Eagle?'

'I deny that I wrote any letter to her and I did not see her on the Tuesday.'

'Take the fragments of the letter in your hands.' Sir Charles took the witness to each recognisable cipher. He suggested that the passage ran 'Will you meet me in the Bar of the Eagle tavern?' The witness said he could not assist; it was indecipherable.

'Assuming you wrote the letter on the 10th, the name of the Eagle was known to you?'

'It was not known to me.'

'Yet that was a public house where you had been with the woman on the Saturday?'

'Yes.'

'Then explain to me why you did not know the name?'

Mr Justice Grantham addressed the witness: 'Yes! I thought you had lived in the neighbourhood all your life?'

It was an awkward moment. Wood was in deep water. It did not imply that he was guilty, but it was unlikely that he was being truthful in this small matter.

Marshall Hall jumped to his feet. 'No, my lord! Not in the neighbourhood of the Eagle. The Rising Sun. It's a long way away.'

'It's a mile,' snapped back Sir Charles. He went on to suggest that the next words were 'near Camden Town Station'. Then, passing to the word 'Wednesday', he suggested that that referred to 11 September.

'Can you mention anyone else with whom you would be making an assignation on the night of Tuesday, 10 September, except Phyllis Dimmock?'

'It is unusual for me to make appointments. I have many friends and could easily have made an appointment on that night, but I did not do so.'

'Look at the word "ill"; has that no reference to your father's illness?'

'That may have, one could imagine that. It is imagination that we are writing round these words. There are able men here who might write something else.'

'You deny having sent Dimmock anything but the postcard? It is your explanation that you wrote many things in her presence?'

'Yes.'

'You had been in her company three times, and three times only, before the night of 11 September?'

'Yes.'

'Were the things which you wrote in her presence given to her?'

'Yes, they were amusing phrases and sketches.'

'Now does that burned fragment fulfil either of the descriptions which you have just given to us?'

'No. I cannot say what it is. I can make neither head nor tail of it. That is honest.' Honest or not, it seemed most inadequate. It was admittedly in his writing, yet according to him was reconcilable with nothing he had ever written or given to her.

'Does not that letter make an appointment for 11 September – an appointment which you kept?'

'No! It does not. You, Sir Charles, have written that round it.'

'The jury shall be the judge of that,' was the quiet reply. 'Let us turn to your meeting in the Eagle. Miss Raven is quite wrong in saying that you stayed twenty minutes after Lambert left and that you and the girl left together?'

'Phyllis bade me goodbye in the corridor. Perhaps she calls that leaving the bar together.'

'You pledge yourself that you said good-night to her in the corridor of the public house?'

'Yes.'

'I put it to you, did you not go home with her?'

'No, I did not. I have never been home with her.'

'You were never there in the early part of the morning of the 12th?'

'No, I was not there.'

'Did you not both completely undress?'

'No.'

'Did you not get into bed with her that night or early part of the next morning?'

'No.'

Sir Charles waited as he framed his question, then with a marked deliberation asked, 'Have you ever had sexual inter-course with Dimmock?'

'It is only to you, Sir Charles, that I would answer that question at all. I should be indignant with the average man.' It was a pitiful answer, but was not going to deflect this prosecutor.

'But still I put it to you.'

'Then I most decidedly did not,' was the answer.

For three long hours the witness was pursued relentlessly. Every word, every phrase, every intonation in the prosecutor's voice was carefully chosen and pitched. Every word, every phrase, every act of the prisoner was scrutinised.

'Your relations with Ruby Young had been intimate in character?'

'Yes.'

'For how long?'

'The whole three years.'

'Did you know she was following a nefarious calling?'

'It hurt me very much when I first found out.'

'When did you find out?'

'Some little time after I met her.'

'You knew of this improper calling for something like two years over which your intimacy extended?'

'Yes. I liked the girl and was prepared to tolerate it.'

His crucifixion was approaching its end. Sir Charles asked him about Ruby Young again.

'Did you give her a ring?'

'Yes.'

'Why?'

'It was something to please her.'

'What is the plain English of that answer?'

'It belonged to Mrs Wood, who had died in the spring. She wished it, so I gave it her.'

The tension in the Court again relaxed as Sir Charles Mathews sat down. It was difficult even now to assess the outcome. Wood had made a bad witness. The air of hypocrisy with which he had cloaked himself was not encouraging. His constant denials that he had had intercourse with Phyllis, his shocked and outraged air, were incongruous when set beside his admission that the sweetheart with whom he had consorted for three years was, to his knowledge, a practising prostitute. It was apparent that he had opportunity to have committed the crime. Only lack of motive made it questionable whether he was a person likely to have committed it. Marshall Hall asked few questions in re-examination.

'Assuming that the letter of which you saw the fragments was addressed to Dimmock – which I know you do not admit – what is the necessity of describing the locality of the Eagle as has been suggested, which is in her immediate neighbourhood? Do you know?'

'No.'

Wood's evidence was concluded. He had blazed a trail and set a precedent for the future conduct of trials in capital cases, but he had blazed the trail badly. Yet this might be a favourable rather than a damning factor. The jury might consider that it was unlikely that a foolish and transparent individual could have committed such a ghastly crime. Only their verdict would decide.

When advocates of the stature and status of Marshall Hall and Sir Charles Mathews are opposed, it is of no little significance who should address the jury first. He who has the last word leaves the last impression on the jury's mind. Excepting when the Attorney-General or Solicitor-General appeared to prosecute, as they normally did in cases of murder by poisoning, the last word rested with the Crown, unless the defence called evidence as to facts. Since evidence had been called by Marshall Hall, he was obliged to address the jury first. (Since 1964 the order of speeches has been changed to give the accused's counsel the last word.)

Marshall Hall began by thanking the jury for the unbroken attention they had given to the case, and acknowledged the debt he owed to Wellesley Orr, an unusual compliment, for Orr had not been briefed in the case. 'I am confident as an advocate,' he continued, 'and I hope I am confident in judging of your natures that there is not one of you, least of all the twelve of you, who dares to say: "That man in the dock murdered Emily Dimmock." On your verdict hangs the life of a human being; your verdict must be a verdict on the evidence. And the evidence you have had from the Crown has been produced upon a principle of selection. That evidence has been edited to an amazing degree; and again I say you dare not, dare not hang Robert Wood on it.' As Marshall Hall spoke he leaned slightly towards the jury; they in turn leaned slightly forward in their seats, the attention which they gave was of that rapt intensity associated with children listening to a fairy story. Every point was pounded into their brains by the advocacy of the KC. To use a phrase coined by a judge in another case, Marshall Hall described with words what was only otherwise achieved by 'the pen of a Zola or the pencil of a Hogarth'.

'What is the evidence in this case?' he asked. 'What is the theory of the prosecution? This case has been presented to you, gentlemen of the jury, as one of premeditated murder, not the action of a moment of passion. The sending of a letter of assignation at a strange place, the commission of the crime, and the providing of a false alibi have all been indicated as suggesting premeditation. Is it possible that if Wood intended to murder the young woman on the Tuesday night he would have introduced his victim to his friend Lambert who happened to come into the Eagle public house, when he knew all along that that same night he intended to do her to death? Would he not have postponed his evil deed?

'There are two kinds of murders; those with, and those without, a motive. A motiveless murder is one done by a practically insane person. I ask you, gentlemen of the jury, where is the motive for this murder?'

He paused as if giving the jury time to answer, then went on: 'I have searched in vain amidst the clouds of evidence for some motive, some weapon, something which would nail Robert Wood to the fateful facts.'

He asked the jury to take into account the temperament of the accused, his overweening vanity, which made him take the responsibility of denying his associations to retain the respect of his friends.

'There is the widest gulf in the world between a man who, finding himself in a mess through associating with women of that class, lies to save his reputation and a person who could commit a murder of this atrocious nature. The false alibi which he arranged with Ruby Young would not have cleared him of the murder. It was merely an alibi to get him out of his connection with the murdered woman.' Marshall Hall had made this point both in cross-examining Ruby Young and in his speech opening the defence to the jury. The practice today is generally to keep an opening speech short, but Marshall Hall's opening speech was much longer than his closing address. It is surprising, however, that he dealt with this aspect in a mere few sentences when closing, since it was, perhaps, his strongest argument in Wood's favour. If Wood had been the murderer and the killing occurred around five o'clock in the morning, it was odd in the extreme that Wood should be setting up a false alibi for 10.30 p.m. on the previous night.

The only evidence to fix the time when the crime was committed was that of Dr Thompson, who said that death was instantaneous and the body was cold and rigid when he saw it shortly after 1 p.m. on the Wednesday. The doctor declared that he could not say definitely how long Emily Dimmock had been dead but, he said, it was several hours, probably seven or eight, putting the crime at between 5 and 6 a.m. on the previous morning. The only other fact available to him, according to his account, was the condition of her stomach, which he said indicated that her death occurred three hours after taking food. The stomach contents are notoriously unreliable as a guide and, if she died between 5 and 6 a.m. this meant that she had had her last meal between 2 and 3 a.m. This in itself seems highly unlikely. Rigor mortis, on the other hand, sets in from three to seven hours after death, and is generally fully established at nine hours. It begins to disappear from thirty-six to forty-eight hours later, so it was clearly present when the doctor saw the body the following afternoon. It is strange that his evidence did not cover this aspect at all. Mathews, for the prosecution, could not, of course, challenge the evidence of his own witness and Marshall Hall would have been exceedingly unwise and even stupid to do so. Dr Thompson was not a consultant pathologist but a local police surgeon and at the turn of the century forensic medical and scientific evidence was less sophisticated than today. Wood had organised a false alibi for the period up to 10.30 p.m. on the Tuesday. If he committed the murder then Dr Thompson had got the time of death wrong. If Dr Thompson had got it right then it pointed most strongly to ignorance on the part of Wood of the time the crime occurred, and so to his innocence. Marshall Hall, however, made little of this in the final address.

With an advocate of the calibre of Marshall Hall it was inevitable that passions would be aroused. Often his was as much aroused as anyone's. By the time he was halfway through an address he was carried completely outside himself. He no longer saw a court; there was only the jury and every nerve within him was strained to impress them with the truth of what he had to say.

'I consider that the prosecution has adopted an unfortunate process of selection. In a case of this kind nothing should be kept back. The evidence of Sharples and Harvey was in the possession of the police two days after the murder. Yet the defence has been left to put those two material witnesses in the box. It is absolutely unpardonable not to have called those witnesses who spoke of seeing Dimmock in the company of a man not the accused on 11 September—'

Sir Charles Mathews sprang to his feet, his arms waving, his gown gyrating round his body. 'I will not allow that to go. I strongly protest against that statement, my lord. I offered to call those witnesses if Mr Marshall Hall wished it—'

'I say—' interrupted Marshall Hall, but Sir Charles was aroused.

'I must stop my learned friend. I will not allow that to go. My learned friend has said in the hearing of the jury that the conduct of the Crown in regard to two witnesses was unpardonable.'

'Decidedly,' persisted Marshall Hall, 'in not putting them into the box.'

'I had hoped that my friend's moderation would have allowed him to keep within bounds, but his immoderation has not allowed it.'

'I am in possession of the Court,' blandly stated Hall.

The Judge endeavoured to pour oil on the troubled waters: 'I quite expected that Mr Marshall Hall would make some remark about the exclusion of those witnesses and that you, Sir Charles, would make some explanation.'

'I do not retract, and I will not retract, that the conduct of the prosecution in not putting those men in the box was unpardonable,' continued Marshall Hall.

'Mr Marshall Hall,' asked Sir Charles, 'did I not tell you that if you desired any witnesses called I would put them in the witness box for you at the close of my case?'

'All I can say is that if that offer was made I did not appreciate it. So far as Sir Charles Mathews is concerned I accept his explanation fully and I unreservedly withdraw my criticism. Had I heard that offer I would have availed myself of it. I have to withdraw. I do withdraw, but had those witnesses been called I would have submitted at the close of the case for the prosecution that they had destroyed their case.'

That Sir Charles made the offer would have been in keeping with the standards and manner of conducting prosecutions. That Hall was wrong in his strictures was equally clear, as he acknowledged. Was it, however, the mark of a great advocate to introduce this attack on the Crown and then have to apologise? Certainly it interrupted the flow of his address and must have broken into the concentration of the jury on his cogent and attractive arguments.

The prosecutor pacified, Marshall Hall went on: 'The only iota of evidence against Wood is that of the witness Mac-Cowan. . . . If any of you had some poor suffering animal to kill I do not think you would kill it on that sort of evidence. The prosecution here is in a dilemma, either to believe MacCowan or the officials of the electric supply department. It is idle to ask you to believe that the clocks of the department selling electricity to the Borough Council were wrong. If Wood is to be convicted, it will be necessary to show that even the clocks are wrong. . . . Has ever such evidence been called for the Crown before on a capital charge? Even the clocks are to be put on one side in order to convict this man of murder?'

He passed on to describe Ruby Young – 'that poor, unfortunate, wretched woman' – and castigated her statement that Wood had a peculiarity of walk as a gross and vindictive lie invented as revenge for the questions put to her in the magistrate's court to show she was a prostitute. 'I claim that the calm and unruffled demeanour of Robert Wood immediately after the murder was based on a calm and unruffled conscience. Where there is a bad alibi it is broken to pieces by a good cross-examiner. Not only is there in this alibi the evidence of Wood's father and brother, but there has come forward to the rescue the old gentleman who lives in the basement, one of the most honest witnesses ever called before a jury, just as Crabtree is one of the finest specimens of the opposite.' As he drew to a close the beads of perspiration stood out on his forehead.

'I have nothing more to say than to remind you that the responsibility is yours now. If you are satisfied that the man standing there, on the night of 11 September murdered Emily Dimmock, although it breaks your hearts to do so, find him guilty and send him to the scaffold. But if – under the guidance of a greater power than any earthly power making up your minds for yourselves on the evidence – if you feel you cannot honestly and conscientiously say you are satisfied that the prosecution has proved this man to be guilty . . . then I say it will be your duty, as well as your pleasure, to say, as you are bound to say, that Robert Wood is not guilty of the murder of Emily Elizabeth Dimmock.'

As he sat down a murmur of approval ran through the Court. It was in general a magnificent speech, worthy of the high reputation of its speaker.

By comparison the reply for the Crown was unimpressive. Perhaps Sir Charles thought his case warranted little argument. He might have said in reply that the failure to postpone the 'evil deed' because he had met Lambert may have been foolish, but was not exceptionally foolish. Suddenly faced with Lambert, there was little to do but introduce him and Wood might have thought that what was done in the dead of night would have little relation to what was done early in the evening. True, it was a trivial mistake, but had the positions been reversed it is not to be doubted that Marshall Hall would have told the jury that it was small mistakes like that which enabled murderers to be caught. This is only a minor and obvious argument which might have been urged, but Sir Charles made no delay with such matters. He appeared to be more concerned with defending the conduct of the prosecution in not calling Sharples and Harvey; in condemning the marking of MacCowan's door because he gave evidence. But, since he conceded that the marking was not attributable to any fault of the defence, it is difficult to comprehend where its relevance arose. He urged the jury to accept that Wood's association with Dimmock was of long standing and that Wood had lied in the box.

'Do you believe', he asked, 'that the postcard was written in the public house because he was asked to write something nice?' He pointed out that evidence of motive was desirable as assisting a jury to arrive at a decision, but it was not essential. 'You have in the accused a man who is a peculiar man, a man cool and collected, an extraordinary man, whose nerve is such that from day to day when the newspapers were publishing accounts of the murder and he was spoken to about it by his foreman, he preserved his calmness and cheerfulness. It was a cold-blooded murder and the accused is a singular – a very singular man – unnaturally, dreadfully singular, a man with nerves so extraordinary that nothing could move him, nothing, absolutely nothing. When he found that the woman he had been with only a few short hours after he had met her in a tavern had been murdered, he did not blench; no change in his demeanour, not a flicker of an eyelid. When the newspapers took up the tale, sparing no detail, did he tremble? Not a scrap.' It was no lack of ability or power of expression which limited Sir Charles to what some might think an inadequate speech. His last effort was impelling in its directness. As he spoke, his arms gave the appearance of 'a sinister little black raven with flapping wings'. Wood himself had said of him, 'When he described night, one actually saw night, if he described blood, one saw blood.' He was closing his speech: 'I ask you not to act on suspicion but only on evidence. I do not think the police have been quite generously treated. I contend that from the beginning to end they have done nothing which entitled them to be treated other than fairly.'

He had concluded. In essence his speech gave the appearance that, as a result of Marshall Hall's outstanding oration, he now regarded the police as being on trial rather than Wood. But the issue was still uncertain. There was still the Judge's summing-up, and he had been demonstrably against Wood all along. The summing-up has great weight in guiding the decision of a jury, and after that there would be the jury's verdict. Would this man live or die?

News of a sensational case travels fast. When it was known that the trial was approaching its closing stages, a crowd began to collect outside the Old Bailey. A large body of people will congregate in London to watch the absorbing spectacle of a labourer digging a hole in the road; when the attraction is the outcome of a *cause célèbre* – the verdict on a man's life – it is not unnatural that the crowd should be so much greater. As the afternoon wore on the mass of faces grew bigger; before many hours had passed they filled Newgate Street, and stretched well into Ludgate Circus. Special police had been put on to regulate the traffic and the assembly. They stood, patiently, to be apprised of the outcome of this stirring fight, then rapidly drawing to its end, under the gilt figure of Justice.

Inside the Court, the Judge was congratulating the jury on approaching the end of their labours and pointing out that they had been engaged in one of the most remarkable trials in the annals of the Criminal Courts of England. 'It is my duty to tell you, members of the jury, that in these cases it is not a safe test to ask what is, or was, the motive which could have induced a person to commit such an act of murder. We none of us can control, we are not able to control, human thought or feeling, or fathom the workings of the human mind; and you know that from the records of the past many of the most brutal murders have been committed without any apparent motive which would have been appreciated or have any effect upon the mind of an ordinary individual. Therefore, it must not be assumed that because no motive has been shown on the part of the accused, therefore he is not guilty.'

The Judge went on to describe the defence and said that he was justified in saying that the accused had been leading a double life: on the one hand a man of excellent reputation, on the other hand he seemed to have frequented places where harlots resorted.

'The greater the degradation of this poor woman, the greater the degradation of the prisoner in dealing with her in the way he did. I regret that many other young people are leading a similar life and permit themselves so to order their lives as to live together unmarried, and I hope this case will result in opening it to a great extent and will be a warning to them.'

No doubt Mr Justice Grantham had strong views on the matter, but many will wonder what this had to do with a charge to the jury in a case of murdering a prostitute, however meek and affectionate she may have been. Her life was a life and was entitled to protection; by the same token the accused was entitled to scrupulous fairness, devoid of any prejudice generated by his style of life. How it affected the matter that other young people were living in sin was not explained. He continued, 'The case depends entirely on circumstantial evidence. But a large majority of murders in the past have been detected by circumstantial evidence. There is the case of Wade and Donovan which I myself tried at the Central Criminal

Court. In that case, although there was no direct evidence, the men were convicted and subsequently confessed. But it behoves you to be very careful before you accept such evidence and condemn a man to death.' He pointed out that there was no evidence which brought the accused in the company of the deceased at all on the morning of the murder, or after he left the Eagle public house with her on the night of 11 September. He asserted that Wood had lied and been untruthful throughout the history of the case and gave examples from the evidence. 'I do not see', he went on, 'why the Crown should have called Sharples and Harvey' – this was a mild rebuke in the face of Marshall Hall's vigorous protest. 'There has been no explanation of the burned letter. That evidence is very strong against the accused and would justify you in believing Roberts's story. . . . the evidence of Wood himself is remark-able. Had he been as honest as Roberts his story would have been in the possession of the police three weeks earlier.' Why the Judge made the comparison is not explained; he appeared to argue that Roberts had gone to the police; in fact, the police had gone to Roberts. 'His sworn statement that he had never seen Dimmock before cannot be relied on, and those witnesses who said that he had seen her before are more likely to be right. The evidence shows that Wood lied at the beginning, just as he lied at the end. He has never given any information to the police. On the contrary he kept everything he possibly could from them. Here is a poor woman done to her death, with whom he had been in contact within an hour or two of the murder. He says he is innocent: yet he keeps everything from the police and his own brother. . . .'

As the Judge charged the jury, the winter's afternoon turned into evening. It was in keeping with the nature of the happen-ings so often recounted there that the most dramatic moments at the Old Bailey occurred in the late afternoon. The mist seeped through the shutters, permeating the Court, the crowd-ed room lit up by a dull and rather subdued system of lighting, the air pregnant with expectation. It was a tense scene: the lone figures of the prisoner and warders sitting in the dock; counsel and solicitors watching the Judge, then the jury and then back again to the Judge; the jury receiving their direction, sometimes nodding understanding, sometimes wrinkling their brows in disagreement or perplexity; and all the while the smooth, soft, measured tones of the Judge, seated on the Bench, suggesting possible viewpoints for the consideration of the jury, most of which pointed to conviction rather than acquittal.

For one thing was abundantly clear this winter's afternoon: the Judge was indicating in no uncertain manner that he regarded the accused as guilty. His summing-up was so strong that Wood could only be acquitted if the jury were completely to disregard his expressed opinions on questions of fact. Would they? Outside, the crowd was growing and becoming more impatient as minute succeeded minute. Fifty mounted policemen had been called to provide against an emergency. As Arthur Newton listened with trepidation to the deadly summing-up, a police officer whispered to him, 'If there's a conviction, I don't know what will happen.' Nor did anyone else. As the Judge continued, whispers of 'grossly unfair', 'outrageous' and similar remarks were to be heard in the well of the Court. Marshall Hall sat with an air of indignation and outraged feelings, making it plain to the jury from his changing expression how horrified he was at what was being said.

Then, for some reason not then or since explained, a change occurred; the Judge paused, turned his notes, paused again – and went on:

'Although undoubtedly it is my duty to do all I can to further the interests of justice so that criminals are brought to justice and properly convicted, it is also my duty to inform you – to tell any jury – that however strongly animosity may go against him, you must not find a verdict of guilty against the accused unless no loophole is left by which he can escape. In my judgment, strong as the suspicion is in the case, I do not think that the prosecution has brought the case home near enough to the accused—' The voice of the Judge was drowned in cheers from the court. 'Silence! Silence! Silence!' cried the usher, but it was in vain. Cheers. The bursting of long-restrained emotions gave vent to uncontrollable cheers. When the noise had subsided, the Judge with a final direction concerning their duty, and in the silent hot packed Court, said, 'Now, consider your verdict, gentlemen,' and the jury filed out to do so.

It was 7.45 p.m. A chatter of voices broke out in the well of the Court, coughing, movement, tapping fingers. With apparent lack of concern the prisoner sat in the dock* while the reporters feverishly completed their copy and counsel discussed the sudden change in the course of the summing-up. Even now the issue was in the balance. Summing-up, cheers and all other things taken into account, the jury had the final word. What would it be?

The scene was described in the *News of the World*:

When the Jury retired there was nothing else to fix every eye, save the statue in the dock, a statue, as it seemed, endowed with life, untouched by emotion, even when the Jury was considering whether he should go to the scaffold or to freedom. While the Jury deliberated he never turned a hair or moved a muscle.

He sat on like a man deeply interested in a new phase of life; like a child absorbed in a new plaything.

Only in this case his plaything was death. Faces were glued to the glass screen of the dock, wherein sat Wood.

Calmly, deliberately, he sketched during the final supreme moments of this great and unparalleled trial. His life hung by a thread, the thread was actually trembling. But still he sketched with a calm, unclouded face and a thin hand, firm as marble. The growing picture of the Judge was evidently a good likeness. He smiled once or twice, seemingly at his own deftness. This detachment – this absolute, terrible detachment – was inhuman. After a few moments a warder moved silently over to where Wood sat, twiddling his pencil over the background. He tapped him on the shoulder and whispered telling him to stop sketching. The artist looked up sharply, raising his eyebrows. Then he leaned back, glanced at the clock in the gallery and waited developments. On the face of it the most disinterested face.'

Time passed and Marshall Hall expected a long deliberation, but, when at eight o'clock a bell rang and someone said, 'They

---

*Unlike nowadays, it was customary for the prisoner to remain in the dock, instead of returning to the cells, while the jury deliberated.

are coming back,' he feared the worst. A quick return was a bad sign. It seemed inconceivable to him, in spite of all he had done and in spite of the Judge's clear direction, that they could have found him guilty, but a short deliberation was a bad omen.

The jury filed into their box. The Judge returned to Court; the Clerk rose to his feet and the foreman of the jury rose with him.

'Gentlemen of the jury, have you agreed upon your verdict?'

'We have.'

'Do you find the prisoner at the bar guilty or not guilty of the wilful murder of Emily Elizabeth Dimmock?'

'We find him "not guilty".'

Cheers loud and long rent the air, and as their sound, and the news, reached the enormous crowd waiting outside they were taken up from Newgate Street to Ludgate Circus. Wood stood composed, within him a sudden feeling of intense depression, a fainting feeling at the pit of his stomach. He was taken from the Court by Arthur Newton to an hotel in the Strand. As they entered the building a newsboy shouted, 'Ere y'are, sir, Camden Town murder – trial and verdict, read all about it.' Wood already knew. Ruby, misunderstood and persecuted by public opinion, was obliged to leave the Central Criminal Court dressed as a charwoman, for fear of the violence which the crowd might inflict.

So ended the Camden Town murder trial. It settled many things: the innocence of Wood; the advantages of calling prisoners in their own defence; the justification for the Criminal Evidence Act, which made that course possible; and, by no means least, the rehabilitation of Marshall Hall in the eyes of the legal world as an advocate who could still achieve a popular victory. All these things were settled by the Camden Town murder trial. But one thing remained unsettled: who, indeed, did kill Emily Dimmock? Did this trial effectively settle Wood's innocence for all time?

One day many years later, as Marshall Hall was leaving a provincial assize court, he was accosted by a small, happy man.

'I see you don't know me, Sir Edward,' he said.

'No, I'm afraid I don't – please forgive me. I have a terrible memory for faces.' He looked at the man again, at the deep sunken eyes and the long artistic fingers. 'But, why yes,' he said, 'isn't your name Wood – Robert Wood?'

'No,' replied the little man as he turned and walked away, 'it's not, but I'd like you to know I'm doing very well – and I owe it all to you.'